Whole Language

What's the Difference?

Whole Language
What's the Difference?

Carole Edelsky
Bess Altwerger
Barbara Flores

Heinemann
Portsmouth, NH

Heinemann Educational Books, Inc.
361 Hanover Street   Portsmouth, NH 03801-3959
Offices and agents throughout the world

The authors and publisher wish to thank the students from Mark Keppel School who appear on the front cover of this book, their parents, for granting permission to use their photographs, and their teacher, Mary McCawley, for providing the photographs.

Library of Congress Cataloging-in-Publication Data

Edelsky, Carole.
    Whole language : what's the difference? / Carole Edelsky, Bess
Altwerger, Barbara Flores.
      p.   cm.
    Includes bibliographical references.
    ISBN 0-435-08537-9
    1. Language experience approach in education—United States.
2. Language arts (Elementary)—United States. 3. Language
acquisition.   I. Altwerger, Bess.   II. Flores, Barbara.
III. Title.
LB1576.E27   1991
372.6—dc20   90-42804

Designed by Maria Szmauz
Printed in the United States of America
91 92 93 94 95   10 9 8 7 6 5 4 3 2 1

For the teachers (past, present, and future)
of Jay, Gail, Lynn, Erika, Asher, Natasha,
and all the other children

Contents

■•

Acknowledgments

•■•

We are grateful that Janet Binkley encouraged us to develop a much shorter version of some of these ideas (Altwerger, Edelsky, and Flores 1987) into this longer, updated volume. It was Philippa Stratton's, Patrick Shannon's, and William Stokes's ability to see beyond what is to what could be that nudged us to think new thoughts, to improve the manuscript not just organizationally but substantively. We appreciate the care they took in exercising their considerable talents both for critique and support on our behalf. Every author should have such outstanding editorial/reviewing help. Sarah Hudelson helped us straighten out confusing passages in a very early version. Pat Rigg gave much needed advice and support. Alice Christie saved the day—and the file—on more than one occasion when the computer seemed to be eating the work in progress. We thank them all.

Introduction

•••

You know they're different somehow—those teachers at the
group meeting of Teachers Applying Whole Language
(TAWL); the principals who have joined that writers' workshop; the teacher educator who works with the teacher and
children in that classroom analyzing pottery shards; the
teachers whose determination to direct their own in-service
led them to found a nonprofit corporation devoted to spreading "best practice." It's not only what they do in the classroom or the principal's office. It seems to be something about
them. Yet, they don't stand out in a crowd—until they speak
up, that is. Then the difference is immediately apparent.
These people make a reality of the rhetoric about the *profes-
sion* of education. They are confident enough in their professional knowledge about learning and language that they are
not bamboozled into going along with slick "instructional
materials" or school district edicts that contradict their own
knowledge, or long-standing norms that distance the universi-
ties from the schools. They are not only wise in their professional judgments; they understand the theory and research
that lie behind their judgments. Moreover, as they've worked
according to that theory, they have also had their eyes
opened about what stands in the way of the best theoretically
defensible practice, about how the system really works. And
so, with that firsthand knowledge of the politics of education,
they have become *politicized* professionals, working to take
control of their own professional lives. When they speak up in

1

public, it is clear that they know what their general framework is, that they know what backs it up, and that they know what practice fits with it. They are whole language educators publicly demonstrating whole language, showing that, in substance, *whole language is a unity of framework, theoretical base, and congruent practice.*

But currently, whole language is also a "hot label," a bandwagon on the roll. The evidence is everywhere. Entire school districts are declaring themselves "whole language." Educational agencies are now writing "whole language" behavioral objectives. Ever sensitive to such shifts in the market, publishers are trying to climb aboard, offering such oxymorons as "whole language" basals and "whole language" pocket charts for flash cards. And wherever we go we hear statements like the following:

"We do 'whole language' every Tuesday afternoon."

"There's nothing new about 'whole language'; we've known about the 'whole child' for decades."

"We've had 'whole language' in this school before but we just called it the 'language experience approach.' "

"But we've always taught skills in context."

"I've always been a 'whole language' teacher; I've used literature since I started teaching."

So not only is whole language popular; it is also surrounded by confusions. In fact, the confusions make us wonder just what it is that is popular: the idea of whole language? the label? innovation per se?

Educational innovations have not fared well in the United States. With its materialist, consumer culture, the United States tends to "consume" innovations—to gobble the latest new idea, not tasting or digesting the substance, using it up, spitting it out, and on to the next. One remarkable exception here is that long-lasting innovation, the basal reader (Shannon 1989). A more typical case, however, is open education. It was widely distorted so that open space was substituted for openness of ideas, learning centers for learning-centeredness. The final irony is that it was judged a failure even though (because of the distortions) it was never implemented on any broad scale. (Thankfully, a few exceptions still exist: Prospect School in Vermont, Central Park East in New York City, and scattered classrooms elsewhere).

As with open education, in its early years the spread of the whole language label alone had some value. It created a more hospitable climate—a legitimate space—for those who wanted to work with the substance. But there is a dark side to this. Wholesale adoption of the label alone without the substance can *prevent* change, declaring something done before it ever really gets started. Whole language is too good an idea for learners, teachers, and society to suffer such a fate.

Whole language is not only a good idea; it is also a threatening idea for those with a vested interest in the status quo. It threatens because it is *profoundly* different from predominant views about education. As such, it counters the established system so deeply and thoroughly (in premises built into roles, materials, and assessment) that it has the potential not only for affecting learners and teachers in the classroom but for having widespread economic and political ramifications within the huge institution of education. Such a powerful idea is bound to elicit pained reactions from those it threatens with loss of legitimacy, income, or power. And indeed, in the undertones of the bandwagon's rumble can be heard the crack of a backlash. If whole language is to gain strength (or even simply to remain) as a viable alternative, it has to overcome the backlash and also the well-intentioned confusions. We hope this book will be part of that overcoming, and that it will help whole language gain strength.

The best defense against being distorted as a trendy new method, being misrepresented by opponents, and being co-opted by publishers wanting to cash in on a market is knowledgeable teachers. Knowledgeable teachers are also the center of a strong movement. By knowledgeable teachers we mean teachers who know about the language and learning theory behind their holistic preferences, who develop an articulate, coherent framework, who measure their practice against that underlying theoretical framework, and who, as a result, claim full status as professionals—in short, teachers who become *truly* whole language teachers. The example set by whole language teachers is a major contributor to that possibility. So is Goodman's 1986 monograph. But, working against it, as we have indicated, is everything that muddies the water, from practice being called "whole language" that isn't, to published statements (emanating from supporters and opponents alike) purporting to describe it but in fact misrepresenting it. We are writing this book, therefore, not to introduce whole language but to "un-muddy" the concept for people who already know something about it (as well as about other educational stances) but who aren't quite sure how it is different—or even whether it is different—from anything else.

As we will illustrate, a wide range of practices and ideas, rather than a narrow orthodox set, make up whole language. Still, there are some limits. Whole language cannot be defined by everything that goes on under its name. Our premise is that there are core parameters to the idea of whole language. These core parameters are what prevent whole language from meaning whatever anybody wants it to mean.

It seems appropriate to say that misdefinitions promulgated by opponents of whole language are wrong. But what about statements and practices by people—like those we quoted earlier—who believe they are supporters of whole language? What about the idea that whole language is a change in the schedule or another way to teach skills? What about the thousand-item lists of "whole language skills" written by state department curriculum workers? Are we being exclusionary to say these are *not* examples of whole language?

Like much in the theory of whole language, the answer depends on the purpose. If our intent were to describe everything happening in the name of whole language, we would, obviously, need to include everything. But our purpose is not to survey and describe whole language as a "movement." It is, instead, to increase the strength of a professional theory that has the best chance of any for improving education. It is to help clarify the idea, to clear up the confusions and answer some of the questions. It is to help already knowledgeable teachers become more knowledgeable—to help them understand the principled theoretical basis of whole language so they can move beyond simply feeling good about the new goings-on in their classrooms to understanding *why* the goings-on *should* be going on.

In clarifying whole language, we will be using the most well-known sources and prototypical classrooms. These share a set of assumptions—those core parameters we mentioned earlier. Naturally, we have selected the part of the core we consider most important. Other whole language sources might have a different "most important" list, but they would still concur with the substance of what we are presenting here.

Toward accomplishing our goal, we will define whole language and explain its bases, compare it with other educational ideas with which it is sometimes confused, relate it historically to its predecessors, discuss at least one of its distortions in relation to similar distortions in another alternative in education, compare it to a current innovation with which it is compatible, and finally, illustrate it with scenes from whole language classrooms.

Whole Language: What It Is

....

A Brief Overview

First and foremost, whole language is a *professional theory*, an explicit theory *in* practice. That is, it is neither theory divorced from practice nor practice that is blind to its own theory. Consequently, it is not possible to label as whole language a theoretical statement tied to no actual educational practice. Nor is it possible to characterize a classroom as whole language simply by checking off a list of supposedly whole language activities. It is the teacher's stated beliefs, the character of classroom interaction, and the teacher's and students' underlying intentions, the *deliberately* theory-driven practice—not simply the behaviors—that make a classroom whole language.

Whole language weaves together a theoretical view of language, language learning, and learning into a particular stance on education. Other innovations in education have taken similar stances. For example, along with prior progressive approaches to education, whole language prefers learner-focused curricula and holds to a conception of the "whole child," of the active learner, of the classroom as a community, and of teachers who learn and learners who teach. For these stances, whole language owes a substantial debt to John Dewey, Caroline Pratt, Lucy Sprague Mitchell, Susan Isaacs, George S. Counts, and other philosopher-artist-educators, as well as to more recent "ancestors" like Sylvia

Ashton-Warner and Roach Van Allen. Much is shared. Yet there are significant differences. What defines a progressive alternative is not just its stance and the nature of its key underlying theoretical beliefs. It is also what the alternative is an alternative *to*. Whole language is unique, then, not just because of what it advocates for education (its stance) but because of the underlying beliefs and the current historical context that, together, give the stance its meaning. We will return to the issue of historical context when we discuss whole language in relation to its predecessors. In this section, we concentrate on the underlying beliefs—whole language beliefs about language and language acquisition based primarily on relatively recent research and theory building in linguistics, sociolinguistics, and cognitive psychology.

A key whole language belief is that reading and writing are learned through really reading and writing (not through doing reading and writing exercises) and, therefore, that reading and writing should be what goes on in school (Edelsky & Draper 1989). Drills on isolated skills or language fragments are exercises, so they don't qualify as reading or writing; neither do entire stories exploited for the main purpose of teaching some skill rather than for a purpose appropriate to story. Whole language teachers do not rely on material written "for instructional purposes." Instead, they use genuine texts—children's literature, recipes, song lyrics, dictionaries, and so on. But just as activities do not define whole language, neither do texts. Using song lyrics for the purpose of enjoying or learning the song is congruent with whole language premises. Using the same lyrics to teach rhyming words or spelling patterns is not.

The crucial difference between really reading or writing and going through an exercise has to do with purpose and meaning. Whole language educators know that all language events, both oral and written, have *some* purpose and *some* meaning. The question, however, is *which* purposes (and whose) are driving the event and *which* meanings are emphasized. If the child's purpose is simply to comply with the teacher's assignment—i.e., if the work really belongs to the teacher and has no intrinsic meaning for the student—then what is going on is just an exercise. And doing exercises is an extremely difficult way to learn language.

Another whole language premise is that process, product,

and content are all interrelated. While whole language educators are interested in processes underlying reading and writing and knowing, they recognize that it is primarily through products and the events in which products are produced that processes are visible. Moreover, they understand that it is content that the processes "work on." That is, language use and learning are always *about something;* and to the speakers, readers, and knowers, the somethings are what is important. Therefore, whole language classrooms provide content-rich curricula where language and thinking can be about interesting and significant content—both traditionally accepted "establishment" knowledge and also knowledge newly created by students—but most importantly, about content subjected to critical analysis. In fact, it is the critical analysis of knowledge (e.g., in figuring out how the knowledge came to be, what functions it serves, and what other knowledge it had to displace) that helps give whole language classrooms the potential to be transformative.

Still another whole language tenet is respect for and trust of teachers and learners. In this professional theory, learners and teachers are seen as capable of directing their own educational lives. They are active, problem-formulating, problem-solving, social beings who interact in a particular cultural and historical milieu. Their teaching and learning is linked to outside communities, and it is communities they form together and curricula they invent together that support their teaching and learning.

What Whole Language Is Based On

A view of language

In a whole language perspective, it is not just oral language that counts as language. Oral language, written language, sign language—each of these is a system of linguistic conventions for creating meanings. That means none is "the basis" for the other; none is a secondary representation of the other. It means that *whatever* is language is learned like language and acts like language. While each mode (oral, written, sign) has its own set of constraints and opportunities, they all share certain characteristics: (1) they are profoundly social; (2) they contain interdependent and inseparable subsystems; and (3) they are predictable.

Language is a social semiotic system. Whether oral, written, or signed,[1] language is a complex system for creating meanings through socially shared conventions (Halliday 1978). We can talk with others, read texts written by others, write to others, or sign with others because we share a similar system for representing meaning. That is not to say that any instance of language signals one and only one meaning or that language cannot be used in intensely personal ways. On the contrary. A particular oral or written text can evoke a wide range of interpretations. What is socially determined is not specific meanings but the range of *potential* meanings for that community. And that range comes from the varieties of voices, conversations, shouts, and whispers each person has interacted with in the past (Bakhtin 1986). The meanings for texts (for language, actually) are not *in* the text or even *in* the language. Language can only mean what its community of users know—the meanings users have attached to the experiences they have had. When the language community has new experiences (e.g., when satellites send back images of Neptune over television), the range of potential meanings for the language (users) is expanded.

Thus even when a person is alone, perhaps writing only for herself, language is still social in two senses: (1) the conventions are shared with other people; and (2) its use is always associated with other texts, other contexts, other people, other voices. In other words, when people interpret a text they use more than that text. Sometimes with awareness, sometimes not, they relate that text to other texts and to the contexts in which they met those other texts. That explains why different people (with memories of different texts and contexts) can hear the same conversation and disagree on what was meant or read the same book and agree in general

---

[1] We will occasionally refer to sign (language) to remind readers that it too is language. However, because of our own ignorance, when examples are called for in our explanations, we will not be able to offer examples of sign.

but still have unique interpretations. On the other hand, it is because people who speak, read, and sign the same language know the same rules that they can communicate ideas with one another and trust that they will be understood.

Language is a supersystem composed of interdependent, inseparable subsystems. The subsystems of language are (1) the phonological (in oral language), the graphic and graphophonic (in written language), gesture (in sign language); (2) the syntactic; (3) the semantic; and (4) the pragmatic. Each of these is a system of rules or conventions.

The phonological system (of oral language) specifies what sounds are possible under particular conditions in a given language. For example, in English a word cannot begin with the sound made at the end of *song* /ŋ/. And the *p* in *pill* will include a puff of air (i.e., it will be aspirated) while a *p* following an *s* (as in *spill*) will not have that puff of air.

The counterparts of the phonological system for written language are the graphic and graphophonic systems. The graphic system specifies what shapes will count as what letters (e.g., counting dissimilar shapes [*a, A*] as the same but similar ones [*c, d*] as different). The graphophonic system provides rules for pronouncing the spelling system (the orthography). The orthography itself is tied to both the sound and the meaning systems. For example, *medicate* and *medicinal* are both spelled with a *c* (pronounced as /k/ in the first case and as /s/ in the second) because of a similarity in meaning, not sound.

The syntactic system is the set of rules that regulates the structure or shape of sentences, thus determining which sentences will be considered "grammatical" for a particular language community.

The semantic system determines the ways words and sentences can convey meaning, whether a particular linguistic unit even has the potential to mean anything in the first place. When semantic rules are violated, we have the intuitive feeling that something doesn't make sense.

The pragmatic system concerns the connections between aspects of context and all aspects of language (pronunciation, word order, spelling options, choice of topic, length of a turn, etc.), including the ways all those aspects are interpreted. Context refers to the general situation, the beliefs and biases of the listener, the overall text in which a particular sentence occurs, who is speaking, who can overhear, or any other tiny local or huge global condition that might influence the use and meaning of language.

One important aspect of context is a person's purpose for producing or interpreting a text. Reading a novel for enjoyment, for example, results in a different interpretive experience than reading the same novel to perform on a test. Certain kinds of texts (i.e., certain genres) also presuppose particular purposes which, in turn, influence the interpretations a reader or listener makes. For instance, readers will usually approach a front page newspaper article with a different interpretive set and a different purpose of their own (to inform themselves) than they will when they read a limmerick.

For our present discussion, the important point concerning these various subsystems of language is that in real instances of language use, all the systems are always present and interdependent. If systems have been artificially removed (e.g., if the syntactic system has been stripped away, as it is in flash cards) or if systems don't work together (e.g., if the context has been set up so that meanings are not used for appropriate purposes), then even if it looks or sounds like language in use, it isn't. (We will return to the discussion of what makes for language *use* in the section "A View of Reading and Writing.")

Language is predictable. Because language comprises these interdependent systems working together simultaneously, it is predictable (Smith 1971). That is, the systems offer cues to narrow down the possibilities. For example, the orthographic system helps predict the next letter, narrowing the choice from twenty-six equally likely possibilities (e.g., *thr* has to be followed by a vowel or a *y*). But the orthography isn't "acting" alone. The other systems help. If *she should* precedes *thr*, cues from the syntactic system help readers to predict *throw* rather than *three*. Letters that come next are not the only things readers make predictions about. They predict words, sentence types, meanings, and so on. And because all the systems are simultaneously present and working together, readers get cues about later words, sentence types, and meanings from more than just a single system. For example, whether it is the beginning, middle, or end of a story influences the word order. Semantic constraints give cues about syntax, and so do pragmatic ones. Thus, language is redundant, offering multiple cues from many directions, and enabling the language user to predict anything from the next word to the gist of a whole text.

Using the subsystems of language as cues to make predictions is not something language users do consciously or deliberately; they predict without necessarily being aware they are doing so. They do not have to be taught to predict; predicting is not a "skill." It is an inherent part of any language use, just as predictability is an intrinsic feature of language (Goodman 1969; Smith 1971).

Predictability is not a characteristic of language fragments, however. A flash card, missing syntactic and semantic cues, is not predictable; it could be *any* word. Moreover, it is not one-wordness that makes something a fragment. What determines whether a word, paragraph, or even a story is a whole or a fragment—i.e., what determines whether it is an instance of *language-in-use*—is whether all the language subsystems are working together. The contrast between *language-in-use* (i.e., *whole* language) and language fragments will be developed in "A View of Reading and Writing" because it is in relation to reading and writing that people most often confuse fragments with the whole.

Language has aesthetic qualities.   Fields as far afield (excuse the pun, but that is part of the point) as folklore, ethnomethodology, and psychiatry recognize that language has aesthetic qualities of sound, imagery, and graphic design. Rhythm, rhyme, alliteration, multiple ways to spell a particular sound as well as a variety of ways to be ambiguous are just some of what contributes to the aesthetic character of language. These qualities are not added on to language by people who are especially "creative"; they are part and parcel of all language use. And they are what makes language an ever-available object to be played with.

If language is an accessible plaything, its users are also inveterate players. To humans, play—with objects and animals, with humans, and with language—is part of life from infancy. Even if cultures discourage playfulness, even if they designate approved types of and contexts for play, they cannot eliminate the aesthetic possibilities inherent in language—the musicality, design and balance, and symbolism that give pleasure to language users. Thus speakers and writers deliberately play around with rhyming, alliteration, repetitive rhythms, double meanings, imagery, and so on. They also do it inadvertently. And listeners and readers may join in and spin off of some deliberate toying around or they may latch onto and continue some sound play or pun that wasn't intended. Singly (e.g., toddlers in cribs crooning themselves to sleep with their own word substitution "lullabies" [Weir 1962]) or in groups (e.g., fans chanting at football games; people following up on each others' puns [Sacks 1973]; audiences reveling in a speaker's stately rhythms), people use language for the sheer pleasure of it as well as for the "work" it does.

•■■•■■•■■•■■•■■• *A view of language development*

Language is learned through actual use. The world over, babies learn language through actually using it, not through practicing its separate parts until some later date when they assemble the parts and finally use the entire thing. Even though pre-sleep or lone-play monologues may sound much like "pattern practice" ESL drills (e.g., *mommy go, daddy go, baby go, doggie go, kitty go*), they differ from what is normally thought of as practice in several ways: they are *self-generated* and self-entertaining or seemingly aimless instead of other imposed, other pleasing, and work oriented. While they may contribute to language learning, they are more appropriately seen as play than as exercises, just as "I'll be the Mommy and you be the Baby" scenes (in which young children try out roles and act out relationships) are more aptly viewed as imaginary play for immediate fun and learning than as practice for future use.

Moreover, babies do not wait to use language until they have mastered each subsystem (the phonology, syntax, etc.). Though their model of each subsystem may be quite unadultlike, babies use each one (especially the pragmatic system) to make meaning. Even when they babble, employing phonological and intonational features and "calculatingly" placing the babble in social events (e.g., as a "contribution" when others are talking at the dinner table), babies are engaged in language use. And at some point in their development (in some cultures it is at birth; in some it is not until toddlerhood), someone in the environment reciprocates by participating in conversations with the child, taking turns and acting as if the young one were a bona fide conversational partner, able to contribute more on her own than she can. In some cultures, it is the parents, caretakers, or other adults who are the baby's primary talk partners. In others, it is older siblings or other children in the community. Sometimes, adults (having higher status) speak to toddlers only through intermediaries (e.g., directing remarks to an older sibling who then relays the message to the toddler [Ochs 1982]). But no matter who does it, the same phenomenon is occurring: someone assumes the youngster is a meaning-maker and, by assuming, creates the condition for the assumption to be borne out.

Even when babies are just observing rather than being addressed directly (whether in a culture where adults interact verbally and directly with babies or in ones where they don't), they are observing *language-in-use*—language that is *always* embedded in a social context. That is, whenever language is being used, it carries certain relationships along with its surface messages (relationships people have to each other, to the topic they're talking about, to the situation they're in). What babies learn, then, is not just the language itself but all the relationships embedded in the language use they are surrounded by.

Overarching all those relationships, and a major part of what is learned when babies learn language, is what language is *for*. It is clear from ethnographic research on children learning language (Heath 1983; Ochs 1982, 1984), as well as from informal reflection, that babies learn language for something else—for getting or refusing a piece of apple, for investigating how the TV works, for playing make-believe ponies, for making older brother laugh, and so on. Very little language learning is purely for its own sake. And while adults make some efforts to "teach" language (e.g., "say 'mama' "; "say 'please' "; "when Grampa talks to you, you answer";

"don't interrupt"), most adult teaching efforts are aimed at teaching *living*, not language—teaching the young ones how to be good members of that household or community, which includes knowing how to talk to certain family members and when to say what. Of course, the adults use language to do that teaching. And as they teach, the child learns not only how to live in that household (how to eat, what to play with, whom to get help from) but also the *language*—that huge supersystem of pragmatics entwined with semantics mixed up with syntax wrapped around phonology—that was used to do the teaching.

Learning language through actual use is not limited to the acquisition of oral language by babies. All language learners, whether they are learning a second language or a written language, learn by really using language, not by going through exercises or artificial language-like activities. Just as babies learn to talk by really talking, by really asking for more water (not practicing so they can then ask for more when they're older), children learn to read by really reading (stop signs, labels on cereal boxes, picture books) and to write by really writing (keep-out warnings on their clubhouse made from an upside-down box, letters to Grandma, reminders to Mom to get the cereal advertised on TV). They don't learn by "practicing" reading and writing. Nor do they have to wait to use written language until they have "mastered" the skills. Instead, the purposes and functions written language serves become the force that leads to continued development. And the supporting players are the knowledgeable adults and older children who respond to the meaning and intent of children's early reading and writing rather than to the unconventionality of its form.

Language learning is both natural and social.   From a whole language perspective, language learning (oral or written) does not occur because it is innate, nor does it occur inevitably. But if language is an integral part of the functioning of a community and is therefore used as a social resource around and with neophytes, then the learning is *natural* in that it is "incidental" to what else is going on (Lindfors 1987). The social functions of language, not the language itself, are the focus. Indeed it is because people are profoundly social creatures and because language enables them to enact their social nature that it is learned in the first place (Bruner 1983; Taylor 1983).

Long before babies utter any recognizable linguistic unit, language development occurs. It begins with mutual eye contact, with reciprocal smiling, with some "predictable format of interaction" that serves "as a microcosm for communicating and for constituting a shared reality. The transactions that occur in such formats constitute the 'input' from which the child masters grammar, how to refer and mean . . ." (Bruner 1983, 18). In other words, as Vygotsky (1978) suggests, what is experienced first through social interactions becomes internalized and "appropriated" by the individual.

Learning written language is no less social and no less natural. When written language is really used around, in front of, and with the learner, it too is learned as a by-product of use. Whether learning to read and write is achieved primarily through the use of environmental print or storybooks or both, it is the fact that written language functions in social contexts that makes learning it natural. The activity surrounding the use of environmental print and the adult-child interactions surrounding storybook reading provide the social context through which children learn *how* print means and what print is *for* (Altwerger, Diehl-Faxon & Dockstader-Anderson 1985).

There are universals in language learning. Though the social practices around language development differ from culture to culture, there are some underlying constants. For one thing, acquisition occurs through actual use, as we have said. For another, language development is both social and socially embedded. And for yet another, the acquisition process is one of generating and testing hypotheses about language subsystems. Whether a child is learning Navajo or German, growing up rich or poor, urban or rural, that child is generating and testing hypotheses about ways to use the subsystems to make meaning in that community. It is not the case that in one place the underlying process is hypothesis generation and in another it is building habitual responses to stimuli, that in the morning the process is individual and in the afternoon it is social or that on Monday it is the learning of separate parts and on Tuesday it is the learning of a meaning-construing system. Language acquisition is not "eclectic." There is certainly surface variation in learning situations, rate, order of acquisition, and so on, but the underlying process is the same.

Another universal concerns mistakes. What we know when we know a language are the rules for the subsystems and the relations among them. That knowledge is not verbalizable, however—not by proficient users of a language and not by beginners. (Can *you* state the phonological rule that governs when a *t* is aspirated and when it isn't? Though English speakers usually can't *say* the rule, they can *use* it. Their knowledge of rules, in other words, is tacit.) As we have said, language learners hypothesize these rules based on "input" during actual use. They do not learn them through conscious effort or through being directly taught the rules themselves. As they are learning the rules, they continually change and refine them until the rules resemble the adult version. This means that language learning *must* include versions of rules that are not at all adultlike. Mistakes, that is, are inevitable, necessary—and universal.

These universals seem to be easier to accept when the discussion focuses on babies learning a first language. When it comes to reading and writing, however, they are often rejected. In fact, built into instructional materials, assessment procedures, and pre- and in-service advice on teaching methodology are outright contradictions of these universals. Some parents (under pressure from schools, we believe) and all establishment educational sources seem to be unaware of the *hypothesis-generating, total system-building* nature of the language learning process and instead treat written language learning as a matter of accumulating ready-built parts. They act as though written language use were right or wrong rather than closer to or farther from, as though mistakes were bad and avoidable rather than illuminating and inevitable. And they try to directly teach rules (for decoding, spelling, punctuating, writing a topic sentence, etc.), even though to use even a surface version of a supposed rule requires tacit knowledge that cannot be taught. To take just one example, the "rule" about putting a capital at the start and a period at the end of sentences requires that a person have a *sense* (tacit knowledge) of what a sentence is to begin with. The "rule" that "a sentence is a complete thought" doesn't help either, nor does operationalizing this with another rule about subjects and predicates. It is only when people already know the rules tacitly (because they have learned them through use) that they can then understand the verbalized rule for when to use capitals and periods.

A view of reading and writing

We can apply all that we said above about language and language development to reading and writing and completely bypass a separate discussion. After all, as we have been claiming, reading and writing are written language in use; what is true for language use is true for reading and writing. But for many people, reading and writing seem to constitute a separate category. For instance, as we said above, while adults in many cultures treat babies' invented words as something to be remembered fondly, they treat children's invented spellings as something to be overcome. Indeed, people's feelings and ideas about reading and writing are so skewed by their own educational experiences, and those experiences have been so dominated by a small-parts, part-to-whole, learn-through-drill conception of reading that they often have difficulty seeing how anything about language might apply to reading and writing. Therefore, we will single out a few important whole language ideas and repeat them with a discussion specific to reading and writing.

A whole language framework has been developing over the last twenty years. During this time, research in language and language learning (especially early written language learning) has strengthened the theoretical foundations of whole language. Initially, however, the whole language perspective developed out of research into the reading process (Goodman 1968, 1969; Smith 1971).

From a whole language perspective, reading (and language use in general) is a process of generating hypotheses in a meaning-making transaction in a sociohistorical context. As a transactional process (Rosenblatt 1978; Goodman 1984), reading is not a matter of "getting the meaning" from text, as if that meaning were *in* the text waiting to be decoded by the reader. Rather, reading is a matter of readers using the cues print provides and the knowledge they bring with them (of language subsystems, of the world) to construct a unique interpretation. Moreover, that interpretation is situated: readers' *creations* (not retrievals) of meaning with text vary, depending on their purposes for reading and the expectations of others in the reading event. This view of reading implies that there is no single "correct" meaning for a given text, only plausible meanings. This view is in direct contrast to the model of reading underlying most reading instruction and evaluation.

Like reading, writing is a dynamic process as writers discover new meanings. Just as readers do in the course of their reading, writers in the course of their writing continuously revise their own thoughts, meanings, and linguistic expressions as they read their own texts. Like readers, writers too must be making meaning for purposes of their own and must be using all the language cuing systems in that effort. Just as readers read for a range of purposes, writers write to remember, to kill time, to remind others, to entertain, to argue, to think out an idea, to ease anxiety, to create anxiety—always with the intention of creating a message, even if the message is only intended for oneself. In fact, reading and writing—any language use—can serve a seemingly infinite number of purposes (though for any given culture, purposes are limited). There are two qualifications, however, that turn what seems like reading into *fake*-reading, writing into *mock*-writing, language use into *non*-language use. Language cannot be used for *no* purpose and still count as language use. When a parrot or a windup toy "talks," the parrot or toy has no purpose, and the "talk" is not language use. And second, language cannot be used for the sole purpose of displaying proficiency on request. For example, saying something to comply with a request to prove one can pronounce a particular consonant may be speech (sounds) but it is not *talking*. Indeed, there are jokes that ridicule such "talk": Says the proud Grandpa to his neighbor, "My granddaughter here is so smart. Why she's even taking algebra and she's only in eighth grade. Say something to Mr. Smith in algebra, sweetheart!"

As in all instances of language use, readers and writers use cues from all the subsystems (including pragmatic cues about purpose) to construct meaning. They do not use each system separately and then put them together later. As in talking, making meaning and getting purposes accomplished are the main point of reading and writing. If that is not the point or if any of the subsystems are missing or not interacting with each other, then it isn't reading or writing.

Perhaps some examples will help clarify this contrast between (written) language *use* and simulations, between reading and writing and something that only *looks like* reading and writing. Take the difference between a one-word bumper sticker and a one-word flash card. With the bumper sticker, there are *pragmatic* cues (placement on the car) to permit guessing another pragmatic cue—the *genre* (bumper sticker). The genre in turn predicts yet another pragmatic cue—the *purpose*(s). The text could be there to advertise, persuade, or self-identify but probably not to bribe or to show deference. At the same time, the syntactic cue and the graphic cue predict that if the text is a bumper sticker of only one word, the part of speech will be a noun, verb, adjective, or an explanatory particle, but not an article or a preposition. Semantics and orthography interact with the other systems to narrow the range further. The bumper sticker could be *America*, *Jesus*, *Tennis*, *Theater*, but not *through*; *Nevada*, but not *nevertheless*.

What about the one-word flash card? The pragmatic cue is there—that is, the genre is flash card. So is the graphic cue—one word. There are orthographic cues—*therm* will probably be followed by a vowel or a *y*. But there is no syntactic cue to help one decide if it is *thermal* rather than *thermos*, no semantic cue to predict *through* instead of *thorough*. Entire systems of cues are missing. The flash card can be any word. The one word bumper sticker can't. The bumper sticker can be *read*; the flash card can only have tricks done with it—decoding tricks, letter-naming tricks.

Or take a less obvious example—the difference between an assigned report for a legislative committee that will then use the reported data and an assigned report for a law professor who then grades the report. In the latter case, the cuing systems are all present but they don't work together and so what is being produced suffers from decreased predictability. The genre (report) signals the writer is an expert but the professor-audience is more expert than the writer. If the student's purpose is to comply, then knowing that purpose does not help one predict the syntax or the semantics. Because language subsystems are disconnected, this is a writing *exercise*, not written language *in use*. The same is true for filling in blanks in worksheets, finishing Story Starters, going through a chapter to answer questions at the end, or producing business letters that won't get mailed.

The same is also true for reading tests. Even when these tests use excerpts from genuine texts or whole texts (as several new, "progressive" state standardized tests do), the task is not to create meanings but to detect tricks (to discriminate among distractors, for instance) in order to prove proficiency. And when proving proficiency is the main purpose, the entire enterprise becomes an exercise. Tests of reading are prime examples of language subsystems not working together, and therefore not enabling test takers to predict. In test genre, any passage can follow any other, eliminating predictions based on sequence. As long as the material is not blasphemous, obscene, or unpatriotic, anything can appear on a test, eliminating predictability based on topic. Even the best test can only be "read."

And even the most "creative" Story Starter story can only be "written." If students put marks on paper in response to a command to say something (rather than because they have something to say), if they create print without using all the language subsystems in interaction with each other, then the marks are merely masquerading as writing. The activity is written language *practice*, or a written language *exercise*, or a written language *simulation*, or *fake* writing, or "*writing*"—anything except real written language *in use*. When people really read or write (i.e., when they *use* language) they use all the subsystems together. That means their word order fits the genre, their semantic choices fit their audience, their spellings fit their meanings—and all these choices fit their purpose. Unfortunately, proving proficiency (or compliance) is the main purpose for which most students interact with print in school, which means that most literacy activity in school consists of "reading" and "writing" *exercises*.

What usually goes by the name of reading instruction, then, does not constitute instruction in *reading*. At best, it teaches students how to do *reading instruction*. Likewise, in many classrooms, what passes for writing (teachers assigning topics and handing out purposes like "to practice writing descriptive details" or assigning revision and conferring because they are part of district-adopted procedures) occupies so much time that students never have a chance really to write in school. The irony is that if reading and writing are learned through reading and writing, curricula packed full of *exercises* deprives children of time to learn to read and write. Whole language reverses traditional priorities by making time for the real thing.

A *view of learning*

So far, we may have contributed to the general misperception that whole language is only about language learning. It is true: the theoretical bases of whole language do concern language and language learning. But those bases are relevant to learning in general, not just learning to read and write. Moreover, because learning language happens in the course of attending to and learning something else, whole language is necessarily about all the "something elses" in the curriculum. That is, whole language teachers' common beliefs about language learning lead to a certain position on learning in general and on curriculum.

Learning is a social process. As in language learning, learning in general occurs in social contexts and is mediated by others. Even learning in private, by oneself, counts as learning in a social context since it taps into meanings and memories that have been socially formed. Although whole language educators accept the importance of learning through individual interactions with the environment (Piaget 1967), they lean more heavily on Vygotsky's ideas about the social nature of learning (Vygotsky 1978). Whole language takes seriously Vygotsky's notion of the Zone of Proximal Development (Engstrom 1986), which entails stressing the importance of collaborations (between students and teachers and between peers) through which students can transcend their own individual limitations.

Moreover, because learning is social, it obviously involves social relationships (e.g., the power relations implicated in who decides what is to be learned, whose purposes take priority, etc.). That means that what is learned about anything always includes the social relationships that surrounded the learning.

Like language learning, other learning usually occurs in the service of something else. The question is: Is the "something else" intrinsically connected to what is being learned and to the context in which it is being learned? One reason the teaching of isolated skills is rejected by whole language teachers is that in being removed from the contexts in which they would actually be used, the skills lose their intrinsic consequences and become simply pawns in a new context in which the connection between the skill and its function is lost. Thus isolated classroom learning of the skill of map reading, for instance, becomes a pawn for helping students "get someplace" academically, but it does not have the intrinsic consequence of helping them get someplace geographically.

Whole language theory contends that students are best served by an education that accounts for at least three ideas: (1) that the context for learning should take advantage of people's propensity to do/think/know more when they are part of learning communities; (2) that planning for learning and teaching has to account for the social relationships in which the learning and teaching will be embedded; and (3) that what is learned should have some sensible and imminent connection to what it is learned *for*.

Learning is best achieved through direct engagement and experience. Whole language educators have strong roots in this Piagetian and Progressive Education perspective.[2] They believe that everything is learned in mixtures of doing and reflecting (Dewey 1963) and that learners are active participants in their own learning (Piaget 1967). Using Freire's language (1970), education must therefore encourage students to be-

---

[2] In order to distinguish the late nineteenth and early twentieth century movement called progressive education from all other progressive movements in education, we will capitalize the one associated with Dewey at the turn of the century.

come knowing Subjects (with the power to act on their reality) rather than passive Objects (vessels to be filled by the teacher). This means that schools should not be places to learn primarily what textbook writers say that previous scholars have learned; they should be places to do science as scientists do, places to do history as historians do, and so on. (And, of course, *doing* science or history means *using* language rather than practicing or drilling with it. Using it, for instance, to read the work of other scientists or historians and to record the results of one's own work.) Moreover, students' doing should provide them with a chance to introspect on how they went about it so that they not only learn but also learn how they went (and how to go) about learning.

Learners' purposes and intentions are what drives learning. As in language learning, it is purpose that makes the learning occur. Others can participate in the learning by responding to the learner's efforts, by providing more grist for the learner's mill, even by collaborating in the efforts, but they cannot cause the learning. Only the learner's purposes do that. Now, if the sole purpose for the learning is extrinsic to the endeavor (e.g., pleasing the teacher by buying into *her* purpose, getting a good grade, staying eligible for band, etc.), then *what* is learned doesn't really matter. One thing could just as well be learned as something else as long as the teacher pleasing, good grade, or band eligibility is achieved. Not only might what is learned lose its value but the extrinsic purpose might also, so that more and more "motivators" would be needed to prod what becomes an increasingly empty exercise.

Whole language opposes empty exercises. Like Kilpatrick's "project method" of the Progressive Education era (Hines 1972), it tries to encourage learning where the learner's purpose has something in common with the thing to be learned. That means that in addition to responding to the learner's efforts, the teacher's role should be to encourage learners to learn about their own interests, alone and with others. In so doing, the whole language teacher collaborates with students in shaping the curriculum.

Learning involves hypothesis testing. As we have learned from Piaget, hypothesis forming and testing underlies all learning, not just language learning. Whether they're wondering how bees make honey or why countries engage in war, children ask questions about and then hypothesize answers to explain the world around them. Their initial efforts do not match adult answers, just as early invented spellings do not match conventional spellings. The role of education, however, should not be to give children the "right" answers. It should be to provide them with the resources that enable them to evaluate and revise their hypotheses. Learning happens in this process of reevaluation. Whole language teachers support this process by demonstrating learning through actual participation (studying a phenomenon along with a child and offering their own ideas as a co-learner) and through responding analytically but respectfully to children's current hypotheses.

In Summary

Whole language, then, is an explicit theory-in-practice incorporating several views. It sees language as social, aesthetic, and predictable, its predictability derived from interdependent subsystems. It views language learning as profoundly social (occurring between and with people in the course of social life, and including not just the acquisition of language but the transmission and modification of culture). It also looks at language learning as necessarily linguistic (hypotheses are about language subsystems; generating and testing hypotheses ensures mistaken hypotheses or "errors"). The professional theory we call whole language holds that what is true for language is true for written language—for reading and writing. That is, reading and writing are also dynamic and social; they too require the generating and testing of hypotheses, some of which will be "wrong"; they too are learned through actual use. A whole language view of learning also attends to the social and the hypothesizing character of learning as well as the importance of direct experience. As a professional *theory*, whole language not only incorporates these theoretical views, it is bound by them (or by future theoretical views as new knowledge is created).

What Makes Whole Language Different

●●

In the preceding section, we presented a sketch of what whole language is, laying out the main "design features"—the theoretical underpinnings. In this section, we begin to fill in that outline, offering some depth. Here, we attend first to what whole language is by presenting what it is *not*—outright misconceptions about whole language (that it means the whole word approach or "teaching skills in context" or that it is "a method"). Then we locate whole language in time and space. We compare it to some of its historical predecessors—Progressive Education of the early twentieth century and the language experience approach and open classroom of the late 1960s and 1970s. Finally, we try to reveal just a bit more about whole language by looking at it in relation to a compatible contemporary innovation, writing process (or process writing, as it is faddishly called). In making these historical and contemporary comparisons, we will be pointing out overlaps and uniquenesses and, in the process, arguing that the metaphor of a pendulum in education, endlessly swinging back and forth between the same "extremes," is inadequate.

Some Outright Misconceptions

•••••••••••••• *Whole language is not another*
name for the whole word approach

It is understandable that, on first hearing, whole language would sound like whole word. Not only do both labels contain "whole," but both are also presented as having something important to do with reading. And for many people, reading does mean reading words. Given people's own experiences in elementary school and given what counts as current educational practice, such a definition is reasonable. After all, many people have strong memories of being taught to read in school through the adventures of Sally, Dick, and Jane. This Scott-Foresman series, as well as other basals of that time, was based on the idea of "sight-words." The "stories" lacked "storyness" and they depended on extensive repetition of a limited number of words. The goal of these basals was for children to memorize words by repeatedly looking at them and saying them at the same time to establish habitual associations between the sight and the sound. It is easy to see how people fed a Dick-and-Jane diet (or how those who dished it out) might have also ingested the idea underlying these basals—that reading is "getting the words."

But it isn't necessary to have slogged through look-say reading instruction to believe that reading is getting the words. Proficient readers are, in fact, able to read a large number of words, both in context and in isolation. On the basis of logic alone, then, one might infer that proficient reading equals reading *words* (that the surface behavior equals the process), and that one becomes a proficient reader by memorizing an increasingly larger number of words.

Instructional materials and reading tests used today in schools reinforce this logic. Exercises in vocabulary and word attack skills are, obviously, all aimed at increasing knowledge of words. In many schools, the Dolch list is still viewed as the guide for reading instruction; parents are often asked to review these words (on flash cards or lists) with their children at home to support the children's reading development. Though the old Sally, Dick, and Jane basals have been abandoned for more sophisticated, slicker versions, the stories are still mere excuses for practicing reading words in context; "getting the words" is still the underlying goal.

Standardized tests for evaluating reading also approach reading as a matter of word identification. Most of them include a section in which children must identify a list of isolated words. Even informal inventories used for placing children in appropriate reading materials or reading groups use word lists as part of the evaluation procedure. Both common logic, then, as well as ubiquitous school practices reinforce the model of reading as getting the words.

So do influential books. *The Great Debate* (Chall 1967) had (and continues to have) considerable impact on conceptions of the reading process and, therefore, of reading instruction. It was presented as a debate between two distinctly different conceptions of reading: look-say and phonics. Actually, the two are simply variations on a single theme: a phonics approach to "getting the words" and a look-say or whole word approach to "getting the words." The basic premise that reading was a matter of "getting the words" was never questioned. Instead, the only area for debate was how getting the words is best accomplished. Since Chall's book touted that debate as "great" (and fundamental), it set the boundaries on what could be debated. It shut out debates on the nature of the reading process itself and made methodology the only important issue. More than twenty years later, the impact of Chall's book remains; if the only possible argument is which of two methods is the best for teaching people to "get words," and if whole language challenges the phonics method for getting words (never mind that it also opposes the idea that reading is "getting words" in the first place), then whole language must be another name for the other method.

The notion of reading as word identification (whether accomplished through a whole word or a phonics approach) is based on a behaviorist view of language and oral and written language acquisition. (See Harste, Woodward, and Burke 1984, chapter 5, for an excellent review of the behaviorist position.) Because that view creeps into even some of the progressive alternatives we will be discussing later, we will discuss the behaviorist position at some length here. According to behaviorists, language is composed of discrete, separable, and measurable parts. The relationship between the parts and the whole is cumulative; that is, the whole is the sum of its parts. Letters or sounds add up to words, strings of words combine to make sentences, sentences add up to paragraphs, and so on. The individual parts in isolation retain the same characteristics that they have in the whole.

Behaviorists characterized meaning in the same way. The meanings of larger units of language are composed of meanings of smaller parts added together—the meaning of stories is the sum of the meanings of sentences; the meanings of sentences are composed of the meanings of the individual words. So, from a behaviorist perspective, "reading" *words* is a crucial building block to reading anything else; and identifying word meanings is considered the foundation for identifying meanings of larger texts.

The traditional behaviorist position on language learning is that it is largely a process of learning the component parts of language (sounds, words, word combinations) through habitual exposure, imitation, and reinforcement. Presumably, associative bonds that link words to their referents and to each other enable children to build language from the bottom up. Words, in this view, are simply sequences of sounds that have the capacity to refer. According to Miller's (1973) critical analysis, behaviorists see meanings of words as directly or indirectly related to their referents. That is, the meaning of the word *chair* derives from its association with the object chair or one's memory image of the object chair (Fodor, Bever & Garrett 1974). Learning words in oral language, then, is a matter of imitating spoken words and associating them with their meanings (referents) through repeated exposure and reinforcement of correct attempts.

Written language, in this same behaviorist tradition, is not really viewed as language at all, but is roughly considered to be speech written down (Bloomfield & Barnhart 1961). Reading is therefore a matter of converting print back to speech (either overtly or internally). More precisely, reading is seen as a process of associating printed words with their oral counterparts. Interestingly, in this behaviorist account of reading, meaning lies outside of reading per se and gets assigned only after the printed word is converted to speech. The meaning of a whole sentence or text is the sum of the meanings that are associated with each individual word.

Although this behaviorist account of reading is based on long-abandoned conceptions of language, it persists as the underlying assumption of both the whole word-oriented and the more phonics-oriented basals. This explains why schools place so much emphasis on oral vocabulary development as a prerequisite for reading in general, and on introducing new vocabulary prior to reading particular texts. If a word must already be in the oral vocabulary for it to be assigned a meaning after it is converted to speech, then "getting words *into*" the oral vocabulary must be a priority in reading instruction. And if the meanings of larger units of print are dependent on correctly identifying and assigning meaning to each word, then reading must be error-free. To be error-free, the vocabulary of learners' reading material must be carefully controlled, and learners must master the identification of words in isolation. This mastery is achieved through repeated exposure to, and then selective reinforcement of, correct print-sound pairings (in the whole word approach, the print consists of words; in phonics, the print may be single letters or letter clusters). This is the rationale for the use of flash cards in a whole word approach to teaching "reading." It is also the rationale for regarding error-free reading of words (whether in isolation or in sentence-length "contexts") as a valid means of assessing reading ability. Meaning per se receives very little attention in a whole word approach to reading. Getting the words—and getting them right—is the principal goal. Meaning is supposed to take care of itself once the words are "got."

Whole language is based on an entirely different set of assumptions about language and language learning. Learning language is not the learning of words (and other discrete parts) through imitation, habitual association, and reinforcement. It is a process of deducing rules about the systems underlying communication, of making predictions about how language works, and of testing those predictions in the process of using language to get on with living (Harste et al. 1984). There is now overwhelming evidence that language learning cannot be explained by an associationist model of imitation and selective reinforcement (Bruner 1983).

Whole language represents a major shift in thinking about the reading process. Rather than viewing reading as "getting the words," whole language educators view reading as essentially a process of creating meanings. (See the development of this view in the writings of Kenneth Goodman [Gollasch 1982] and Frank Smith [1971, 1986].) Meaning is created through a *transaction* with whole, meaningful texts (i.e., texts of any length that were written with the intent to communicate meaning). It is a transaction, not an extraction of the meaning *from* the print, in the sense that the *reader-created* meanings are a fusion of what the reader brings and what the text offers. Readers indeed use word boundaries and lexical features as cues, but they also create meaning with many other cues—syntax, semantics, and pragmatics (including the reader's purposes and what the reader knows about the author's purpose). Although students who learn to read in whole language classrooms are, like all proficient readers, eventually able to "read" (or identify) a large inventory of words, learning words is certainly not the goal of whole language.

But even in relation to word meanings and the learning of words, whole language's transactional model is sharply different from the whole word method's behaviorist model. In a transactional model, words do not have static meanings. Rather, they have meaning *potentials* and the capacity to communicate multiple meanings. Word meanings change depending on the circumstances of use and the history of literacy the language user brings to the setting (Harste et al. 1984). Learning a word means learning the meaning *potential* for that word—the possible meanings connected with various social settings. Words are not learned in isolation (on flash cards or lists or in oral vocabulary drills) but in the contexts of their use. Knowing the word "table" means knowing its meanings in context: for example, "table the discussion," "check the water table," "table and chairs." Experience with words in social and functional contexts is thus crucial to the learning of words.

Syntactic, semantic and pragmatic contexts (including the language user's background experiences, interpretive set, and understanding of the social situation) determine the specific meaning any word will have in a particular case. This is true for both oral and written language. As an example, consider the various meanings of the words *Mary, had, little,* and *lamb* in the following sentences:

1. Mary had a little lamb.
   Its fleece was white as snow.

2. Mary had a little lamb.
   She spilled mint jelly on her dress.

3. Mary had a little lamb.
   It was such a difficult delivery that the vet needed a drink.

(example adapted from Trabasso 1981)

As this example shows, when people read they create *tentative* texts, assigning tentative in-text meanings constructed on the basis of interpretations of the larger context. The behaviorist notion that texts derive meaning from the bottom up—that word meanings are sequentially accumulated to produce a text meaning—simply cannot be supported. There are no context-free, static meanings of words when language is actually *used*.

Meaning, in fact, does not reside in the print itself at *any* level. The print provides only the text potential (Harste et al. 1984; Rosenblatt 1978, 1985). When people read, they turn that potential into an actual instance, creating details of meaning that must be inferred from, but do not appear in, the printed cues. Young readers can develop serious misconceptions about the reading process (and, therefore, what they are supposed to be doing when they read), if they are directed to extract the meaning of the following basal story from the printed text itself.

PAINTING DAY

Fog was over the city and a light rain came down. It was a cold winter afternoon. The boys and girls had just come back to the room after lunch. Some children walked into the room with wet umbrellas and wet hats. They put them away and sat down. "This is a good afternoon to paint," said Mr. Grant. (source unknown)

There are no words informing us that this is a school, that Mr. Grant is a teacher or perhaps a principal, that the children put their wet garments in a cloakroom or in lockers or maybe over a counter. Clearly this text has the potential to mean these things, but without the school experiences (and schemas) that readers bring to the interpretation of the text, these meanings could not be created. Meaning, then, is a dynamic entity, created for texts in situations. Meaning is not in the printed words themselves.

Whole language and the whole word approach bear very little resemblance to each other beyond the use of the word "whole." They are based on vastly different theoretical premises regarding language, language learning, and the reading process; have completely opposite goals; and represent different instructional orientations. Though a move from phonics-based instruction to a whole word approach may constitute a surface change in method, it takes a fundamental shift in *perspective* to move from whole word to whole language.

•••••••••••••• Whole language does not mean teaching skills in context

This misconception is even more understandable than the one equating whole language with the whole word approach. Thinking and talking of education, learning, and teaching in terms of "skills" is endemic. The popular view of what one does when teaching language is that one teaches skills—pronunciation skills, sentence-forming skills, listening comprehension skills if one is teaching "oral language development" or a second language; decoding skills, word attack skills, comprehension skills for the teaching of written language (DeFord 1985; Harste & Burke 1977). The correspondingly popular view of language learning is that what is learned is skills—not just skills in any order but skills in a hierarchical sequence.

An even more general assumption is that if it is possible to identify subskills (e.g., the subskill of comprehension) in the proficient performance of any complex activity, then those subskills should be taught directly and separately. Tests of separate skills invade education to such an extent that they ensure that the idea of separate skills remains unquestioned,

and that the importance of the parts will precede and out-
weigh the importance of the whole.

Other sources add to the confusion. For instance, educators who are trying to understand what whole language
means often mistakenly misinterpret Goodman when he says,
"Language is actually learned from whole to part" (1986, 19).
After all, it seems so logical. If, up until now, they have been
presenting words, then sentences, then stories, Goodman
must mean they should start with stories and work back to
words. And since whole language teachers do teach the "me-
chanics"; and since they do talk about the "parts" of language—letters, words, sentences, paragraphs, punctuation,
spelling, and so on—the parts clearly matter. It must be (or
so the reasoning goes) that those parts should instead be
learned *after* the whole story is presented.

Aside from those who labor under this particular misun-
derstanding, other beginners who do not yet know new ways
of talking about the more substantive changes they are making refer to what they are now doing as putting formerly isolated skills into a context or as "integrating skills." And to
add even more to the confusion, thoroughly whole language
teachers whose goal is to promote the development of knowledgeable, critical, literate people, who do not turn "whole-to-
part" into a mechanical reversal of skills instruction, and
who know that teaching *skills* is not their objective at all,
nevertheless sometimes use the term "skills in context" to
describe their programs. They do so knowingly and self-
protectively. After all, when these teachers are in districts
that permit only skills instruction, saying they teach "skills
in context" is a good survival strategy that allows them to
continue to act on their whole language understandings.

The misconception goes beyond thinking that whole language is about "skills." It is also a case of trivializing the notion of "context" by shaping it with a "small parts" mold.
"Context" is usually seen as a background "part" rather than
as the crucial medium for language use. Sometimes "context"
is reduced to meaning merely the verbal setting (e.g., the
story as background for the sentence, the sentence as background for the word). It is almost never understood that context itself can be *created* by language use.

A body of experimental research buoys up this belief in

separable small parts, in context as a background variable, in part-to-whole learning and teaching, and in meanings residing in behaviors, parts, and print. Buoys up or legitimates—not *proves*. The difference is crucial. To *prove* the belief, the research would have to *question* the existence of separate skills. But it doesn't; it *assumes* it. In fact, it builds it right into the study. Thus, the experimental tasks in research that support small-skills beliefs are tasks involving separate skills—tasks that bear little resemblance, it must be noted, to real-life activity. And special materials (texts and tests) used in this research are designed to highlight specific separate skills, so the materials are stripped of the cues offered by real-life materials-plus-context. Such distortions rarely bother experimental researchers or "consumers" of the research. Instead, this is seen as research business as usual (which it is). Research can shed light on what it questions, not on what it fails to question. The research that supports a belief in separate skills does reveal something about various details that grow out of its premises (e.g., whether children learn a particular separate part better if they are given extrinsic rewards), but it does not address the built-in premises themselves (e.g., whether language does indeed consist of separate parts).

The same premises that underlie skills research also undergird school policies, instructional materials, standardized and criterion-referenced tests, government funding policies, teacher accountability schemes, and on and on—with the same attendant treatment. Attention is given to how the premises are executed (how word attack skills are best learned; how comprehension skills are best taught). The premises themselves (that written language consists of word attack and comprehension skills) remain unquestioned.

Beginning from different premises—and focusing intently on their own and others' premises—researchers such as K. Goodman (1969); Y. Goodman (1980); Goodman and Altwerger (1981); Ferreiro and Teberosky (1982); Harste, Woodward, and Burke (1984); Edelsky (1986); Teale and Sulzby (1986); Flores, Amabisca, and Castro (in press); and many others have conducted research that supports the idea that language learning is a simultaneously social, conceptual, and linguistic process. These researchers have shown that, right from the start, language learning is the development of a supersystem whose component systems are inextricably interwoven. In other words, language learning—learning to read and write—is not a matter of learning skills in context; it is a matter of learning this supersystem of conventions that governs all the interactive social, conceptual, and linguistic contexts for one's community. This is the case whether one is learning conceptions of the nature of the system itself (Ferreiro & Teberosky 1982; Harste et al. 1984), changing hypotheses about various language subsystems (Edelsky 1986), appreciating the function of print (Goodman & Altwerger 1981), learning cultural ways of knowing that are embedded in early oral interactions (Ochs 1984), or acquiring culturally appropriate norms for oral- and written-language use (Heath 1983).

The whole language view is that reading (or writing or oral language) is something that cannot be segmented into component parts and still remain reading, that any "component subskill" of reading (e.g., decoding) used when one is not actually reading (e.g., when one is doing exercises in decoding) works differently than it does when someone *is* really reading. Moreover, the subactivity is not merely the behavior. Decoding, for instance (like all other subactivities of the total activity of reading), has a role to play in the total activity: it interacts with other subactivities; it engenders consequences. If the role it is supposed to play and the relationships and interactions it is supposed to have with other subsystems are taken away, what is left is only the behavior—meaningless in itself. It would be as if one could learn to ride a bike by practicing balancing, steering, and braking separately from one another without ever getting on the bike and riding it.

Authentic use is the condition under which learning to read or to talk (or to ride a bike) occurs. And in authentic use parts are not discrete; they influence each other. (Steering that bike is not separate from pedaling either!) Thus syntax influences phonology, permitting a reduced vowel when *can* is a part of a verb (*the garbage /kan/ go over there*) but not when it is a noun (*the garbage /kæn/ is over there*). Syntax influences graphophonics so that initial *th* + vowel is voiced for function words (*this, that*) but voiceless in content words (*thing, thistle*). Semantics controls syntactic parsing in such sentences as *Flying planes can be dangerous.* Pragmatics affects word choice and syntactic options (*Would you mind holding this for a minute?* vs. *Hey, c'mon, help. Can't you see I'm having trouble?*) Pragmatics is what permits variation in orthography (*lite/light; through/thru*). It should be noted that the direction of influence is from high to low; the higher system is required in order to make a decision about the lower. This is just the opposite of a "skills" paradigm, where there is a hierarchy that begins at the supposed beginning—the smaller units and the lower levels.

A major whole language goal is to help children *use* (not sever) these interrelationships among higher and lower, "top" and "bottom" systems. The means for achieving that goal is to engage children with authentic texts (versus textoids, as Hunt [1989] calls them) and in authentic reading and writing. So while a whole language framework intends that children become "skilled language users," it does not advocate that children "learn language skills." There is a world of difference between these two. To become skilled language users, children learn language conventions, sometimes incidentally, sometimes with conscious attention to particular cuing systems. Whole language teachers *do* teach children how to spell words they are using, *do* teach appropriate punctuation for letters children are writing, *do* teach strategies for sounding out particular combinations of letters under particular circumstances. But neither this teaching nor the children's learning follows an externally devised, school district–mandated curriculum sequence. What one child learns is not necessarily what the other children are learning, and most importantly, what is taught or learned is triggered by what the children need for the language they are actually *using* at the time. That is, to become skilled language users, the focus of both teacher's and children's activity is whatever purposes the children themselves are trying to accomplish. By contrast, to learn language skills, children work on exercises according to a curricular sequence, and above all, the focus of teacher's and children's activity is the skill.

"Skills" and being skilled are clearly not the same thing. Altwerger and Resta (1986) have shown that many proficient readers cannot do skills exercises, while many poor readers can. That is, the activity of performing divisible subskills may have little or no relation to the indivisible activity of reading. It is the latter activity that interests whole language people.

Whole language is not a method (or a package or a program)

Nor is it an addition to an eclectic grab bag of educational resources. Erroneous ideas about eclecticism, however, are inextricably tied to the error of thinking whole language is a method or even an instructional package. And *that* error is one promulgated by many quarters. First there is the current general tendency in the culture to use metaphors that turn human life into machines or packages (e.g., the human mind as being programmed, human emotions as the playing out of old tapes, the human body as a machine, public figures as commodities). It is not surprising, then, that a new idea about education (when education, too, is treated metaphorically as a commodity) would be reduced to a similarly mechanical or commodified metaphor.

There is also a strong tendency for people to assume that what shows (in whole language, for example, that could be heavy use of literature or journals) is all that matters, that the essence is the surface behavior—the methods—rather than the underlying meanings.

Then there are concrete statements from authoritative sources. Documents such as state reading guides describe whole language as "one of many methods." Publishers of instructional materials advertise "whole language basals" and "whole language phonics programs."

Teachers' own professional education may contribute to categorizing everything that is important as a method by separating theory from method and then aggrandizing method. Teacher educators are not immune to the conventional wisdom that learning means learning skills. They too are often victims of this separate skills mentality, which translates into an emphasis on methods. Therefore, they conceptualize teaching as skills for doing—skills in planning lessons, in managing the classroom, in implementing a curriculum (often planned by others)—as enacting *methods*. And they create teacher education programs that separate the methods courses (the hows) from the theory courses (the whys) and thus hide the intimate connections between the two. Then, at the most critical part of the program—student teaching—they focus almost exclusively on method, rarely even examining, let alone emphasizing, the theoretical assumptions deeply embedded in methods. (A notable exception here is the teacher education program called Project S.T.A.R.T. at the University of Pennsylvania. See Cochran-Smith, Garfield, & Greenberger [1989] for a description.)

Once teachers are on the job, the pressure intensifies to see all of teaching as method. Teachers are not expected to question the theoretical assumptions of the "tools" they are handed (district curriculum guides, published materials, evaluation instruments); indeed, they are chastised if they do so. The expectation is that all that someone needs to know about these tools and methods is how to use them. The central question asked in the most common teacher evaluation instruments is not what theory guides teachers' work; it is what skills do they have with the methods they are using.

And now the method-plot thickens. Adding to the belief that all is method and to the belief in skills (skills of teaching, skills of reading) is a near lusting after the eclectic. Whether they are afraid to take a stand, want to avoid offending, or simply want to be inclusive, educators tend to resist thinking in terms of this *or* that, preferring instead an eclectic this *and* that. If they were to see methods as theoretical, then they would see that not all are theoretically compatible; they would have to exclude some on theoretical grounds. But if everything is "just a method" then it can be included in an eclectic repertoire with other methods. Eclecticism redefines theory-blindness as a virtue.

When method becomes all-important, then any slight variation in method takes on more significance than it is worth. For example, teaching with word banks and teaching with phonics activities *are* different *methodologically*, but not *theoretically*. Both methods grow out of the same separate skills theory about language and language learning. This does not mean that whole language educators ignore individual children's preferences or needs. On the contrary. But in devising different strategies for different children and different situations, whole language teachers make two important distinc-

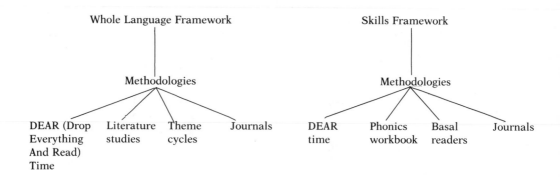

FIGURE 1 • (Altwerger & Flores 1986)

tions. First, they distinguish between the level of framework (or paradigm or theory) and the level of method (or practice or strategy). Second, they select from the "method" level what is congruent with the theory level. By contrast, a belief in separate skills and the primacy of method, going hand-in-hand with obliviousness to the level of framework (one's own and any others), leads people to reduce everything (including whole language) to method. Such a reductive mistake has two negative consequences. First, it decreases the likelihood of reaping hoped-for benefits from borrowing "a little bit of whole language" without making the prerequisite theoretical change (doing exercises with a basal and doing exercises with a piece of literature still amounts to doing exercises). And it also damages whole language by diminishing overall understanding of the framework.

Figure 1 schematically represents the contrast between the level of framework and the level of method. (The number of methods displayed is, obviously, only a tiny fraction of existing or yet-to-be-invented methods.) Equating whole language with a method is an error in level of abstraction. It is true that methods are always theoretical; that is, they always stem from some theoretical orientation. And theories always have direct or indirect methodological implications. But theory and method are not interchangeable. As Figure 1 shows, journal writing and basal readers are part of methodology. Neither is an underlying theoretical framework. Skills paradigm and whole language are theoretical frameworks. Neither is a method. Frameworks are at one level of abstraction; methods at another. But refusing to look at the theory embedded in method prevents teachers from fully understanding what they are doing.

So let us repeat: whole language is not a method. Nor are there any *essential* whole language methods. Some methods are easily made congruent with a whole language perspective. Self-selected reading of literature, literature studies (Edelsky 1988; Eeds & Wells 1989; Peterson & Eeds 1990), theme cycles for studying content (Altwerger, Resta, & Kilarr in press; Altwerger & Flores 1986), student-as-ethnographer projects (Heath 1983; Wigginton 1979), interactive journals (Flores & Hernandez 1988; Staton, Shuy, Payton & Reed 1988), writing workshop (Calkins 1986), shared reading of "big books" (Holdaway 1979), and creating a literate environment (Loughlin & Suina 1982) are just some of the practices or methods with potential to fit a whole language framework.

However, none of these is *essential*. A classroom in which children spend the whole year raising chickens and selling the eggs (including writing statements to persuade school board members that such a curriculum would be beneficial, reading advice about how to increase egg production, and writing advertisements to increase sales) could well be a whole language classroom. So could a classroom that emphasized science projects and excluded literature. So could one in which children never wrote personal narratives but attended exclusively to art and drama (writing to publishers to obtain releases for play readings and staging the school's own gala arts fair). Or one where teacher and students together spent the year investigating and acting on a political issue in the community.

If no method is essential to whole language, neither does any method *guarantee* whole language. That is, a classroom with literature studies, writing workshops, journals, and so on is not necessarily a whole language classroom. What *is* essential, what makes a method "whole language," are certain principles or beliefs, because that is what whole language is—a paradigm, a framework in action. It is this frame that underlies how the teacher handles error, how the teacher treats text, how the teacher expects conventions to be learned. It is this frame that would, thus, either permit children to read genuinely in the course of raising chickens or consign them merely to doing reading exercises even with a bounty of children's literature. In other words, the "same" method used by someone with a different set of beliefs becomes a different method.

As is apparent from Figure 1, many methods can be used with either a skills or a whole language framework (it is the teacher's belief that gives meaning to the method). Some materials and activities, however, simply do not fit a whole language view. For example, activities that fragment language or materials written for the instruction of separate reading or writing subskills conflict with whole language beliefs by definition. If they are used as the teachers' manual suggests, even the most "holistic" phonics materials and basal series all entail *simulations*, not real reading. By eliminating some subsystems, artificially highlighting others, or ensuring that the learners' purpose must be compliance with an assignment, they can be nothing but exercises. Thus the basic whole language belief—acquisition through *use*—is violated. The only way a basal reader technology or a phonics program could fit into a whole language classroom would be for children to use them as data; for example, as documents in social studies projects on the history of changes in school reading materials and how they reflect wider societal changes. They could not be used for practicing or learning supposed subskills of written language, including comprehension as a subskill, and be congruent with whole language beliefs. (In whole language, if there is reading, there is comprehension; if there is no comprehension, there is no reading. Comprehension is not a subskill.)

Clearly, all methods (and all materials) are not based on or used with the same premises; that is, interactive dialogue journals did not grow from the same theoretical soil as flash cards, and a teacher using a poem to teach synonyms is operating from a different and contradictory theoretical ground than one who reads the same poem to children to delight in the sound play. Adamant "eclectics" ignore these contradictory theoretical grounds, but they get tripped up on them just the same. Though they may be unwelcome, basic contradictions do exist. The theoretical assumption that reading consists of separate skills contradicts the theoretical assumption that reading does not consist of separate skills. Even though people value eclecticism and want to believe in it, at the level of deep underlying beliefs, *there is no eclecticism*. Instead, knowingly or not, people hold one underlying view and shape lessons, materials, interactions, and goals to fit that view (Harste & Burke 1977). Teachers with a skills viewpoint may hold literature study sessions (a practice that is potentially congruent with whole language), but they will inevitably turn them into skills-based "high-level" reading groups; they will use the sessions to teach skills (albeit "high-level" skills) rather than to argue the author's intent. Like a liquid, practice takes the shape of whatever belief-container it is in (Browne, personal communication 1985).

If eclecticism only meant having a large repertoire of materials, modes of interacting, scheduling options, and so forth, then we would applaud eclecticism. After all, whole language teachers are eclectic in this sense; they are not tied to only one way of interacting, one schedule, one type of material, one way to treat a topic. They know and use many methods, many ways to teach. Indeed, they are particularly sensitive to the need to vary their approaches with different children for different purposes. However, "being eclectic" usually means something else when people tout its virtues—something more like holding one unacknowledged, unexamined underlying theoretical position, borrowing typical practices from conflicting positions while unwittingly and inevitably distorting them so they fit the one unacknowledged position, and thus fooling oneself about the supposed variety. In contrast, whole language teachers are conscious of and examine their own underlying beliefs and the theoretical assumptions buried in all methods and materials; they deliberately make sure the theory embedded in their methods matches the theory they espouse. They know that what they are about is not perfecting a method to add to a collection of other methods; it is coming to understand with greater depth and clarity the non-eclectic, unified, principled whole language framework they work from.

Some Historical Predecessors of Whole Language

The picture is filling in—the theoretical outline starts to have some shading from contrasts with outright misconceptions. Now we begin to sketch in the background.

Whole language is one of many attempts in recent history to alter education. In order to help people understand whole language better, we will discuss it in relation to several of these attempts, each discussion having a different purpose. First, we will relate this current progressive (small p) alternative called whole language to a famous progressive movement of the early twentieth century called Progressive Education. In making this comparison, we will also argue that whole language has the potential to be a liberatory pedagogy. Next we will look at the language experience approach to show the contribution made by that alternative to loosening, but not severing completely, the cords that bind teachers to prevailing pedagogy—the contribution, in other words, to easing teachers into whole language. Then we will focus on open education, using the similarities between it and whole language to highlight a problem unfortunately common to both (the ease with which these perspectives are distorted) and to analyze one particular shared distortion—the study of content.

Progressive Education and whole language

From the late 1800s to the early 1930s, Progressive Education's goals were to help the whole child—mind, body, and ideals—develop as an autonomous being in interdependence with others, either for achieving social harmony (Dewey 1916) or for correcting social ills (Counts 1932). These two themes—the *individual* and *society*—were augmented by others. Progressive Education was *experimental*—children could try out ideas and learn from their results; teachers were to approach teaching with the experimental stance of a scientist. The curriculum was carried primarily through *direct experience* (Dewey 1963). Textbooks and teachers' tellings were indirect, secondary, and therefore inferior, sources. Children's own *activity*, their *work*, was the vehicle for their learning. Real work—and real play (the boundaries were not at all distinct)—consisted of the kind of common, productive activity that constituted the physical reality of life (e.g., wood working, weaving, sewing, cooking, and so on). Work was not to be externally imposed; *choice* (self-initiated activity) was necessary. So was *purpose*. Children were to take part in activity "not because one is told to but because all one's faculties are primed for work" (Pratt, quoted by Antler 1987, 244). They were to pursue their own questions, to study things because they "really *wished* to." Examples of self-initiated projects undertaken because children "really wished to" through Kilpatrick's project method were "catching frogs for our aquarium" and "finding out how taxes are collected at Pineville" (Hines 1972, 147). Progressives were interested in an *integrated curriculum*, but not such superficial integration as using art in a history lesson (Dewey 1916); they wanted the kind of integration in which subjects like geography, history, biology, even reading and writing, would be learned in the course of, for example, selling shop products or printing a newspaper (Pratt, cited by Antler 1987, 240). Experimentation, choice, work, purpose, and so on were characteristics appropriate for education for *democracy*. Progressive Educators believed that the only way to prepare children for life in a democracy was to give them a democratic school experience.

What about language and language learning? How did Progressive Education account for these concerns that are so central to whole language? Though such topics received little attention in many Progressive writings, they were not ignored. Progressives like Lucy Sprague Mitchell thought language was an expressive art medium, that children's language had inherent aesthetic strengths (rhythm, directness, style) (Antler 1987). They wrote that in the course of studying the world, children would learn to read incidentally, just as they learned language incidentally. Dewey argued that language was learned through use and not lessons: "The fundamental modes of speech, the bulk of the vocabulary, are formed in the ordinary intercourse of life, carried on not as a set means of instruction but as a social necessity" (1916, 17). Therefore, language acquisition was the "perfect model of educative growth" (1916, 113–14). And as with all other subject matter boundaries, the "separate" language arts were to blend into an integrated unity with other activity (Shannon 1989).

Doesn't all of this sound like whole language? There is the emphasis on children's purposes, their firsthand experience, hypothesis-generating and testing (experimenting), child-initiated activity, genuine work, a focus on "something else" (the work) rather than on language, language acquisition as a model for education, language learned through use and not lessons, and learning to read incidentally. Is whole language, then, a direct descendant of Progressive Education? *Yes*, the general direction of whole language toward promoting the growth of the individual *within* a community and toward promoting curricula full of purposeful, guided firsthand experience can be said to have come directly from early attempts to "progress" in education.

But on closer inspection, *No*. Important underlying whole language beliefs about language and language acquisition do not have their origins in Progressive Education. Language as predictable through cues offered simultaneously from multiple systems; written language as both social practice and as a sociopsycholinguistic process for making meaning by means of generating and confirming hypotheses; authentic language use as distinguished from exercises on the basis of how purpose is connected to language cuing systems—these basic whole language ideas are not a legacy from Progressive Education.

Even when statements from whole language and from Progressive Education use the very same words, they don't necessarily mean the same thing. Take the seemingly shared language about language. What Colonel Frank Parker (whose influence appears in Dewey's work) meant when he said *language arts should be integrated* was that grammar should be learned through the writing of sentences and short compositions (Shannon 1989). And when proponents of Progressive Education wrote about *language being learned through use and not lessons* and about *language acquisition being a model for education*, they meant something different from what whole language educators mean by the same phrases. Dewey's point, for example, in contrasting learning language by lessons versus use was not to argue that tacit conventions for language cannot be learned through direct instruction. In fact, he went on to say they *could* be—that "the mother tongue" could be "corrected or even displaced by conscious teaching" (1916, 18). Instead, he was putting language in a category with other signs of social class and was arguing that the best teacher of manners, morals, and values (i.e., of "breeding") was the "unconscious influence of the environment." And when he proposed language acquisition as the model for education, he was referring to the development of speech organs (not to abstract rules of language) and the need for a "social medium" to direct the development of those organs. He was not refuting direct instruction; he was rebutting Rousseau and the idea that education should be totally laissez-faire. While whole language educators appeal to language acquisition to argue against trying to teach language directly, Progressive Educators appealed to language acquisition to argue against *not* doing any teaching at all.

Reading, in Progressive Education, was to be learned incidentally or from child-created "reading leaflets" (Monaghan & Saul 1987), which sounds much like whole language. But what Progressives meant by reading was not creating idiosyncratic yet socially constituted meanings through the use of (written) language; it was understanding words. And the best way, they thought, to learn to understand words—read aloud or silently—was through a whole word approach (Monaghan & Saul 1987).

The question of ancestry, then, is not so easily answered. We have already replied both yes and no. When we said yes, we were referring to some important positions on education and learning that whole language shares with Progressive Education. (It also has much in common with other later progressive movements, like the language experience approach and open education, which we will discuss later.) When we said no we have been referring so far to differences in underlying theories about language and different meanings for similar statements.

But there is more to it than that. Just as important as the theoretical differences are the differences in historical times. Obviously, we mean much more than just differences in dates on a calendar. To be progressive in education means to change, to move forward, to go *toward*. That also implies that one is moving away *from*. That is, whole language, like all its progressive predecessors, means what it means in large measure because of what it is supposed to progress *over*, what it is an alternative *to*, what circumstances it is meant to *change*. Alternatives, that is, have their opposites built right into them.

So instead of looking closely, let us back up and look at the entire panoramic scene—Progressive Education in the early twentieth century as compared with whole language in the late twentieth century. Each of these progressive perspectives on education was in opposition to particular prevailing ideas about education, children, and society, to particular educational practice, and to particular societal circumstances.

The Progressive school of the late nineteenth and early twentieth century was, by today's standards, a refuge in a cruel setting. Urban conditions were deplorable; political machines were exceedingly powerful and corrupt; privilege and cronyism rather than merit or "neutral" business accounting procedures were what ran social institutions. Millions of desperately poor immigrants, escaping far worse conditions, arrived with "foreign" ways and "radical, un-American" ideas. Their children trudged off with the children of the American poor to put in twelve-hour working days in firetrap factories and mines. These (and all other) children, the prevailing thinking went, were born as blank slates, onto which a recognized body of discrete facts and moral lessons was to be written.

But there were other winds blowing, too, around the turn of the century. Hope was in the air. Early capitalism was expanding. The immigrant came not just with a few pitiful parcels but with a heart full of dreams. People were more than fodder or cogs; they were unique individuals with minds, reason, experience, feelings. American Progressive Education was part of a larger Progressive political movement that hoisted this modern figure—the individual—onto center stage to play off the other modern "main character," the environment. Instead of accounting for people's successes or failures by appealing to their inborn individual nature, one could appeal to their experience with environmental nurture. Thus muckrakers exposed one sordid story after another but they and other social reformers also presumed that if the social environment were improved (through scientific rationalism), individuals could flourish. Freud was developing ideas about how inhibitions harm the individual. Thorndike was measuring individual reactions to show that ignoring differences among individuals was also harmful.

Progressive Education took its starting point and its direction for alternatives from what was happening at the time. We cannot understand the Progressive emphasis on child-centeredness, on "freeing creative energies" and creating "autonomous individuals" without setting these ideas against the (Freudian) inhibited child or the child whose individual (Thorndikian) abilities were ignored by faceless schooling. We cannot understand the Progressive concern for direct experience and their fear of books and lectures from authorities without taking account of the way lessons were usually hammered in for rote memorization—and didn't "take." We must consider the Progressives' advocacy of learning through work and occupations—occupations that were homey, small-townish, or even pastoral—in light of seven-year-olds working in urban factories and the struggle to enact laws against child labor. The Progressives' promise of an education that would provide social harmony has to be understood against a backdrop of worry over "outworn moral traditions" and "radical foreign ideas." With its faith in scientific rationality and Protestant-styled civility (Popkewitz 1987), Progressive Education was to erase what were considered outmoded or foreign ways in order to supply the lower classes with the tastes and sensibilities that would permit them social mobility. No wonder business interests supported Progressive Education!

Until, that is, the advent in the early 1930s of the social reconstructionist branch of Progressive Education. The Great Depression was felt in empty pockets and empty stomachs; it was seen in empty stares. Unlike the earlier Progressives, when the social reconstructionists claimed schools should prevent the perpetuation of social inequality, they were not talking about the "unequal" tastes, traditions, and moral sensibilities that might be barriers to social mobility or social harmony. They were talking about having schools be instruments for "building a new social order" (Counts 1932), for changing an economic system that was built on great inequalities and boom and bust cycles. No wonder business support vanished.

"Child-centeredness," "experimentation," "individual ability," "free expression," "social harmony," "new social order"—the ideas important to Progressive Education (indeed Progressive Education itself) got their meaning from their historical context. The same is true for whole language.

In the late twentieth century, we are in a period of multinational corporations, service economies, "wild" economic activity (e.g., hostile takeovers)—a period of "late capitalism." It is a time when people talk increasingly of a permanent underclass, a time when few hopes are held out to those on the short end of the stratified society stick. More and more, we live media-mediated lives, interpreting not just public figures but ourselves through the lens of TV sitcoms, commercials, and sound bytes, and experiencing increasing alienation ("amusing ourselves to death," as Postman [1985] put it). Not for nothing has the current era been called "the me decade." The advent of Yuppies has accompanied an exaggerated selfishness in public policy; on a grand scale, profit and greed have become the ultimate motivators.

As in the early part of the century, however, there are crosscurrents. A general move toward holism has begun to appear in disciplines from physics to medicine to linguistics to education. Increasingly, people try to offset alienation in a search for relatedness and meaning.

Meanwhile, the current conventional view in education is to see children as unprogrammed hardware (a hi-tech version of the blank slate), perhaps with a preference for certain "learning styles." The predominant purpose of education is not transmitting facts and morals or uplifting the spirit but training in skills. Teachers are now being systematically de-skilled and de-professionalized (Apple 1983). Not so they return to the *un*professionalism of a century ago, but so they go "forward" to the lesser power of technological skill *without* autonomy. In fact, skill in using "teacher-proof" curricula and materials written by others is increasingly and cynically being passed off as professionalism. And "skills" have become the new one-size-fits-all descriptor. (Singles advertise in personals columns that they have "communication skills." Employers look for someone with "people skills." A woman who was arrested in Phoenix for locking her baby in a car on a 110-degree day acknowledges she could learn more "parenting skills.")

"Skills" is certainly what drives prevailing educational conceptions of language and language learning. And language and language learning appear to be the motors for educational practice. They take up most of the school day. They use up much of educational budgets. Most important for our argument here, they are the bases for testing and ranking students, teachers, principals, and schools. Indeed, never in recent history has such an arsenal of language-based weapons been used against people with such efficiency. In teacher accountability schemes based on student test scores, minimal competency requirements that push minority students out of school, ability group placement (and thus differential access to higher quality literacy experiences), and tracking throughout school careers (and thus lifelong social stratification), separate language "skills" are used to give social inequality the illusion of being fair and deserved. Never before have responses to tests of supposed language skills constituted such an all-encompassing admission ticket to "an economy with limited seating" (Giroux 1983).

As with Progressive Education (and all other progressive movements in education), we cannot understand what whole language means without recognizing its context. Whole language takes the form it does—putting at its very center a focus on language and an opposition to a "skills" view of written language—because in the current historical context, language has become a major weapon. We cannot understand whole language's refusal to break language down into bits unless we know how breaking it into bits currently functions to track and oppress people. We cannot understand what a refusal to define literature in terms of grade levels means unless we see that refusal in contrast to the stranglehold of a basal technology suffused with "levels" of all kinds. Unless we acknowledge a current context in which individualism has run amok, we cannot fully appreciate why whole language insists on redefining the individual language user as a social being—why it insists on seeing intelligence and reading ability, for example, as activities people accomplish together (largely through talk), rather than as "traits" given to individuals. We cannot understand whole language's insistence on teacher autonomy without understanding how current attacks on that autonomy are a culmination of a generation of de-professionalization.

Without accounting for the differences in their respective contexts, we cannot understand how or whether statements like "promoting individual growth and interdependence," "encouraging children's expression," and others that show up in both Progressive Education and whole language are related. As Fleck said, any statement is always relative to other statements, to ways of thinking and to funds of knowledge at particular times among particular people (1979, 38–39). Progressive Education and whole language are no exception.

Because whole language is anchored in this particular period with all its characteristics, it has a unique potential to be a liberatory pedagogy. Here is what we mean. Whole language educators view schooling as profoundly social. They also believe it is necessary to think critically about the world, to pose as well as solve problems. They understand whole language theory's insistence that problem posing and critical analysis are necessary ingredients of all learning. Therefore, they offer issue-rich content to encourage critical thinking rather than packaged materials (embodying dominant ideologies) that supposedly teach "critical thinking skills" for solving trivial hypothetical "problems." Other key theoretical beliefs underlying whole language (for example, that texts always have multiple interpretations and that learning is an active process) also promote pluralism and increased democracy.

These beliefs and practices help students develop as individuals who can participate critically in current society. But still other beliefs give whole language its potential to be *transformative*. The belief that language is to be learned through authentic use and that language is primarily used for something else opens up classroom schedules. Huge chunks of time usually devoted to exercises are freed for projects in which students can analyze social issues like the systemic injustice and inequality that affects all our lives. We are not saying most whole language educators exploit this potential. Most, in fact, do not engage students in acting on, demystifying, and transforming sociopolitical reality (Freire 1970). But their theory at least permits it.

And what makes whole language truly revolutionary is not just the built-in potential for curriculum rich in critique. It is that built-in potential *coupled with what whole language is an alternative to.* Whole language eliminates the grouping for reading and the tracking that ensure unequal access to "cultural capital" (i.e., certain texts, vocabulary, knowledge, analyses). It devalues the major language-based devices for stratifying people. It makes teachers the authors (not "deliverers" or "managers") of curriculum. In other words, it helps subvert the school's role in maintaining a stratified society.

Thus, moves to replace language-skills-based texts with more theoretically adequate and "authentic" evaluation devices are insufficient. Unless they are coupled with efforts to eliminate their stratifying function, they will not be "progressive." Instead, they will simply be better, richer, and therefore less easily criticizable means of perpetuating inequities.

Between its *actual* subversion of particular means of oppressive ranking in school (leading to even more oppressive stratifying in life) and its (unfortunately often unused) *potential* for critique, whole language could well be a "pedagogy of resistance and possibility" (Aronowitz & Giroux 1985). Despite important similarities to other progressive movements that came before, it cannot be understood *in terms of* what came before. Conditions are different—and it is those conditions that give it meaning. Except at the most general level, there is no pendulum of educational innovations swinging endlessly back and forth. Each innovation has its own meaning because of its stance, its theoretical base, and *what it is in opposition to.* Progressive Education was not ahead of its time. Whole language is not a return to another time. Each is *of its time*—in every sense.

Language experience approach and whole language

The language experience approach is another forerunner of whole language. Its contexts have also shaped its changing meanings over a nearly fifty-year history. Our point this time, however, will be to look not at those contexts but at the considerable contributions of the language experience approach.

We will try to help people understand whole language better by examining what teachers had to learn in order to become language experience approach teachers and what they still have to change in their shift to whole language.

The language experience approach is the umbrella label for a pedagogy more precisely divided into "language experience approach" to teach beginners to "break the code" and "individualize reading" for later literacy instruction (Hall 1976). It became a distinct approach in the early 1940s under the title *Learning to Read Through Experience* (Lamoreaux & Lee 1943). In its evolution over the years, it gave up getting children ready for reading "controlled vocabulary readers" (Lamoreaux & Lee 1943) in favor of teaching them to read period; and it shifted from a focus on reading to a focus on communication (Allen 1976). As we discuss its contributions and its contrasts with whole language, however, we will concentrate on the language experience approach of the 1970s, since that is the version more of our readers might have actually experienced themselves.

The backbone of the language experience approach is the following often-quoted set of propositions:

> What I think about, I can say. What I say I can write or someone can write for me. I can read what I can write and what others write for me to read (Allen 1964, 9).

What was new about this approach is embedded in that quote: "the natural language of learners" was to be a "basic ingredient" of the elementary school experience (Allen 1976, v). Reading was treated as personal and individual, based on whatever language varieties a child brought to the situation of learning to read. Along with other language activity, it had purpose and dialogue at its center (Peterson 1981). The label itself grew out of a school-based research project question: "Of all the language experiences available for study in the elementary school years, which ones have the greatest contribution to make to reading?" (Allen 1976, v). Twenty experiences made the grade. Eventually, these were grouped into three strands: using one's own language to develop language (e.g., listening to stories, discussing experiences, and dictating stories); making use of the language of others (e.g., reading whole books, organizing ideas); and studying components of language (e.g., expanding vocabulary, studying words).

Prototypical language experience approach classrooms were well supplied with literature, literacy tools (e.g., all kinds of paper and writing implements), and art materials (clay, paint, wood, fabric). They had science centers, cooking corners, musical instruments, globes and maps and measuring tools, and sometimes live animals. They were "rich environments." And they were papered with charts—class experience charts, personal language charts, charts of classroom rules, work charts, reading skills charts, and so on. Visitors to language experience approach classrooms saw children writing books, choosing what material they wanted to read, spontaneously talking with others about their reading, and having individual conferences with the teacher about books they had chosen. They saw teachers taking dictation from children or discussing and writing down children's "key words"; they watched children doing exercises with words and sentences from their dictated stories. Visitors saw children working at the various centers where their work in science, cooking, or mapping often included reading and writing. And sometimes, they were invited to join in the language play—the singing, punning, riddling, choral reading, rhyming, and chanting—that was common in these classrooms. (Descriptions of language experience approach classrooms can be found in Allen 1976; Hall 1976; Peterson 1981; Stauffer 1975; Veatch 1978; and Veatch, Sawicki, Elliott, Barnette & Blakey 1973.) Even in classrooms where the language experience approach was used only for reading and where it did not influence the rest of the curriculum, children chose their own reading material, wrote or dictated their own stories, and had individual conferences with teachers about their reading.

In order to teach using the language experience approach, it was necessary to give up treasured beliefs and sacred practices that make up established reading pedagogy. Language experience approach teachers had to (and did) work through and give up the belief that reading had to be taught through basal readers—or through any other texts written specifically to teach reading. They had to give up the idea that all children had to be instructed through the same texts. They had to give up the assumed sequence that children must learn to read before they write. They had to give up grouping children for reading. They had to learn that children's own purposes were of major importance in their reading. They had to learn to prefer children's naturally occurring language over the stilted language of controlled-vocabulary readers. They had to learn to put meaning before form. They had to learn to value individual children selecting their own reading material—even, sometimes, their own activities in other curricular areas. They had to learn to know and love children's literature and see its central role in a school reading program. They had to learn that different children could be engaged in different activities at the same time; they had to learn to give up directing the entire class and begin trusting individuals.

These were no small lessons! If language experience approach teachers had not learned them, they would not have been able to put aside basals; they could not have permitted self-selection of trade books; they would not have been able to encourage children to write their own texts. These lessons made a major contribution to whole language in this sense: teachers who learned them found the road to whole language that much easier.

Ironically, what was missing from the language experience approach (a pedagogical approach focused on language) was a strong theoretical framework about just that: language. The language experience approach of the 1970s was not based on a developed theory regarding the nature of language, language acquisition, or the reading process. It made some use of structural linguistics, and it referred to children's acquisition of vocabulary (appealing to studies of size and type of vocabulary and high-frequency words). But it did not account for either the revolutionary ideas of Chomsky or Halliday in linguistics, the counter offer by Hymes in sociolinguistics, the whirlwind of research activity in child language, or the developing sociopsycholinguistic model of the nature of the reading process.

In fact, reading was rarely defined in language experience approach statements. When it was, it seemed to mean getting a message from print (assuming, that is, that meaning is *in* the print) (Hall 1976). The backbone set of propositions quoted earlier (what I think I can say; what I say I can write, etc.) presumed a relationship between oral and written language in which written language was a secondary system "translating" speech into print. The "level" of written language acquisition, therefore, depended on what a child had acquired in oral language. Reading, that is, had to be built on speaking.

Because written language was seen as a translation of oral language, the language experience approach advocated using transcriptions of children's own talk as their primary beginning reading material (Allen 1976; Veatch et al. 1973). Language experience approach teachers took dictation, writing down children's orally rendered stories verbatim. With the idea that reading (rarely defined) entailed knowledge *about* reading, language experience approach statements suggested that teachers offer skills lessons. Thus, after a child's experience was put to use in dictation, the transcription might then be used to teach word attack or phonics skills. Or after working with Key Words, children might be encouraged to find words with similar beginnings, to cut up words, to find rhyming words, to make word banks, and so on (Allen 1976; Veatch et al. 1973). In line with suggestions for learning about separate language components through exercises, and because there was no theoretical reason for not doing so, language experience approach teachers were sometimes advised to supplement children's literature with instructional materials designed for systematic teaching of reading skills (Allen 1976; Hall 1976; Peterson 1981; Stauffer 1975).

Though the language experience approach made it relatively easy to shift to whole language, it did not make it inevitable. To make that switch, language experience approach teachers must still reexamine much of what they have already been doing in light of a new theoretical frame. They must still come to understand that much of their language experience approach instructional activity was right not simply because it was humane but because it had a strong theoretical justification. They must still learn what that theoretical frame can do for them: that it can help them *see* what they couldn't see before, that it can help them *intervene* (so their interventions do not interfere), that it can help them *participate* ("let *us* discuss" rather than "let me help *you* discuss").

On the way from language experience approach to whole language, teachers learn that language is social, predictable, redundant with cues, reflexive. They learn that language learning is social and that it occurs through use. Language experience approach teachers becoming whole language teachers learn that reading is not a matter of getting the meaning in print out of the print. It is a transaction (Rosenblatt 1978, 1985) in which print offers only potentials for meaning. Readers use these potentials to create the particular meanings we call texts. Teachers moving to whole language learn that oral and written language systems are structurally related, but one is not an alternative symbolic rendition of the other. Moreover, written language learning need not wait for oral language acquisition. According to whole language research, people can learn vocabulary, syntax, and stylistic conventions directly through written language (Edelsky 1986; Harste et al. 1984; Hudelson 1984).

Armed with a coherent new theoretical framework about language and language acquisition, language experience approach teachers who become whole language teachers change some details of their practice. They no longer write down children's speech in the same way. In the language experience approach, taking dictation assumed that composing occurred prior to transcribing (i.e., even fluent writing was seen as a primarily mechanical process of taking dictation from oneself). But from a whole language perspective, meaning making occurs during the act of writing (Smith 1982). Taking dictation, therefore, deprives language learners of a key context for making meaning—the act of writing. It also deprives them of the opportunity to make the full range of hypotheses—about graphics and orthographics as well as about semantics, syntax, and pragmatics. Therefore, when a child wants to put a story on paper, the whole language teacher rarely sits down and takes dictation; she urges the *child* to go write it down.

Language experience approach teachers who become whole language teachers continue to write down speech and read it aloud as they write. But now it is often the teacher's speech, not the child's, that the teacher writes and reads aloud (e.g., when the teacher is responding to a child's journal entry in front of the child, or when the teacher is slowly transcribing onto big chart paper, reading aloud, and pointing out word boundaries or letter formations on a collaboratively generated list children will later use to help them remember). Even when it is a child's spoken ideas that the teacher transcribes, the language experience approach teacher who has become a whole language teacher now does not worry about getting the talk down word for word. She tries instead to find good functional reasons for writing down the talk in the first place (e.g., to remind children of their jobs for the day or to record the results of a brainstorming session). Whole language teachers use transcription to demonstrate how written language works, not to provide children with a text that represents their own speech sounds. They presume that children create hypotheses about how language works from seeing it in operation. And seeing it in operation means not only seeing it produced but also seeing how it functions in the life of the classroom.

Another change language experience approach teachers make in their practice when they become whole language teachers is that they give up "systematic" (i.e., separate) skills instruction through exercises that focus primarily on words. They also give up the occasional use of commercial materials written for such instruction. Whole language theory acknowledges that metalinguistic knowledge about components of language is part of written language competence. But it disputes the following: that such knowledge is a prerequisite for using written language; that such knowledge is best gained through exercises; or that the word-focus of many exercises aimed at teaching that knowledge is appropriate. In whole language theory, words are not discrete entities. They are crossroads of meaning—the subjective meanings of a person's lived experience intersecting with the meanings of text-in-situation and text-tied-to-other-texts.

With its stated assumptions and suggested practice, the language experience approach was the most advanced, progressive, and comprehensive pedagogy on reading/communication of its time. Its important lessons about what was required (and what was not) for teaching reading paved the way for teachers to learn even more. Many of its practices fit right in with and in fact can be found in whole language classrooms. Some, however, are abandoned; others take on a somewhat different shape. But more importantly, the practices take on a different meaning as teachers make the transition from language experience to whole language. When teachers learn a new underlying framework for understanding language, language learning, and literacy, they make even familiar practice into a new experience.

Open education and whole language

We examined the relationship between Progressive Education and whole language to make a point about how a progressive alternative means what it means and to explain why we claim that whole language has the potential to be transformative. Then we compared whole language with the language experience approach, not simply because the two are frequently confused with each other but because in both the history of education and in many individual teachers' own personal histories, the language experience approach has been a practical bridge to whole language. Now, we look at whole language in relation to another in a long line of progressive movements in education—open education of the late 1960s and 1970s. This time, our purpose will be to examine distortions, focusing primarily on one of them—the study of content. What we want to encourage with this section is a heightened sensitivity to other areas of practice ripe for distortion, and a willingness to take an honest look at the match or the mismatch between a whole language framework and a variety of classroom activity within the growing whole language movement. This section, that is, mirrors the purpose of this entire book: to increase the strength of the whole language *movement* by promoting an integrity that can only come from greater understanding of whole language as a *framework*.

Open education of the late 1960s and 1970s was known variously as open education, the open classroom, informal education, the integrated day, and the British infant school model. It drew direct lines between itself and Progressive Education of Dewey's time (Gross & Gross 1969; Lucas 1976; Nyquist & Hawes 1972; Silberman 1970). Since open education advocated the language experience approach for the teaching of reading, most open classroom teachers also had to unlearn significant conventional stereotypes about literacy instruction. But open education also made its own contribution to progress. Through its reliance on the work of Piaget, it made cognitive development—especially the development of logical reasoning—an object of intense interest. Open classroom educators used Piagetian notions to interpret children's thinking and to help promote children's learning. Whole language inherited open education's serious concern for observing children closely and trying to infer the way the world looks to them (e.g., inferring the [implicit] questions children are asking at any given moment and their reasoning in answering them). (See Y. Goodman [1985] on kidwatching.)

Ideally, open classrooms were the richest of environments. They had big building blocks (even through upper elementary years), kilns (not only clay), well-equipped cooking and baking corners, and machines to be dis- and reassembled. Focused on the development of logical (scientific-mathematical) reasoning, they were loaded with plants, bones, rocks, insects, mealworms, chemicals, and other resources for exploring the natural world. Live hamsters, guinea pigs, rabbits, and snakes were common; in some open classrooms, children raised chickens and kept dogs. Teachers were not just in the background (Bussis & Chittendon 1972). They were ingenious and spontaneous facilitators, provisioners of the environment, and resource persons. The classroom itself was often organized around learning centers; blocks of time for rotating through centers alternated with time for free choice. While what seemed to capture children was the topics they chose or the "stuff" they worked with, what was important to adults in open education was "process." They were particularly interested in such cognitive processes as categorizing, inferring, identifying patterns, analyzing, and evaluating. In fact, they often planned for and explained children's activity and their own in terms of these processes (Brearley 1972).

Clearly, open education and whole language share many features of practice. They differ, however, in much the same ways the language experience approach differed from whole language. The lack of a developed theory about the nature of language, language acquisition, and literacy permitted open educators to treat reading and writing as subjects and to use exercises for teaching reading and writing skills. Open education (and language experience) also tended to emphasize the learner as an individual, individually choosing topics of study or selecting from the options the teacher offered at learning centers. The relative emphasis in whole language is more on the side of the learner as a social being, participating in a community of learners during small-group literature study, peer writing workshops, and collaborative projects for studying content. Congruently, in observing children and trying to understand their thinking, a whole language framework tends to rely more on Vygotsky than Piaget, putting more emphasis on the social and historical character of thinking and learning.

We said at the outset that whole language is both a perspective and a movement. So was open education. As with growing movements generally, both of them are (or were, in the case of open education) subject to considerable distortion. Classrooms were called "open" when the only change was in the size of the space—the same traditional curriculum was taught to large numbers of children, but now in big open pods with the walls torn down. In the name of open education, some classrooms were organized around "centers" that were nothing more than round tables hovered over by mobiles where children worked on ditto sheets (round tables must have seemed more "open" than rectangular desks). There were "open" learning modules, "open" packages of instructional kits, even "open" behavioral objectives. We have already mentioned similar distortions of whole language— basals and phonics workbooks being called "whole language," scheduling a "whole language" period of literature or writing into a school day of drills, districts apportioning literature selections according to grade level and providing a standardized set of questions for use in "response" groups, districts mandating that all teachers "use" whole language—as though it were a canned set of procedures for "delivering" a traditional curriculum.

Unfortunately, open education and whole language not only share a propensity for being misconstrued, but they also share the specifics of one particular misconstruing—the study of content. Taking a superficial and somewhat mechanistic view of both "process" and "integrating curriculum," whole-language and open-education teachers often end up trivializing content. Instead of getting children to *do science*, for example (perhaps in theme cycles [Altwerger, Resta & Kilarr in press]), they get them to do science *activities* organized into thematic units. Thematic units are a means for integrating social studies or science topics into the curriculum. They consist of activities organized around one integrative topic (e.g., bears, dinosaurs, spiders, Pueblo Indians, Africa, etc.). By contrast, theme cycles are a means for pursuing a line of inquiry. They consist of a chain—one task grows out of questions raised in the preceding tasks, all connected to an original theme or initiating question (e.g., Were there prehistoric people living where we live now? How do supermarkets really work? How can we get rid of drug dealers on the playground? How can we know how dinosaurs lived if all we have for evidence are pieces of bones?). Of course, offering an opportunity to take part in either theme cycles or thematic units is an improvement over the emptiness of traditional curricula, an emptiness that prompted seven-year-old Jill to complain, "We don't *learn* anything in social studies; we just do sheets"! If we take theme cycles as just one way content study can be congruent with underlying whole language ideas, and if we contrast these with thematic units that were common in open classrooms and are also common in whole language classrooms, we should be able to see differences in the driving force behind each, in teacher and student roles, in major tasks, and in the treatment of the topics themselves.

In thematic units, the topics are used for teaching subjects or skills. In a thematic unit on bears, for example, bears provide the glue connecting reading (bear vocabulary words), math (story problems about bears), science (encyclopedia-keyed questions about bears), literature (stories featuring bears), and so on. In theme cycles, it is just the reverse: sub-

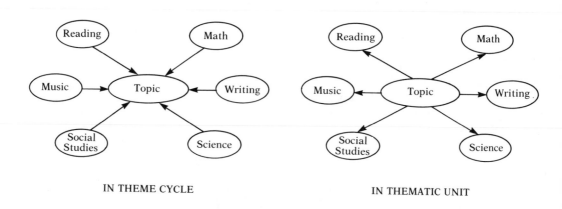

IN THEME CYCLE   IN THEMATIC UNIT

FIGURE 2 • *Relationship of School Subjects to Topics* (Altwerger & Saavedra 1989)

jects and skills (science, math, reading, etc.) are used for investigating the topic, as Figure 2 shows.

In thematic units, music, art, and literature are exploited for nonmusical, nonart, nonliterary ends. In theme cycles, they appear as what they are—aesthetic, cultural (and therefore ideological) phenomena, created under particular social, political, and economic conditions. Paintings, symphonies, sculpture, dance, and literature are not vehicles for teaching fractions or geometric shapes or commas in a series. The whole language theoretical premise behind this contrast is this: *symbolic skills and tools serve content, not the other way around.* We add census data to learn about the population; we do not find out about population totals in order to have a reason to add numbers together.

Since thematic units are skills-driven, they are also full of exercises or strings of "activities" related to one topic. Learning centers are designed to engender interest so that children will be motivated to take part in the planned activities. Theme cycles, by contrast, are not loaded with exercises or "activities." Theme cycle centers that pull together resources in one location are not established to rev up lagging interests but to satisfy already heightened curiosity or to answer questions raised during the pursuit of a topic (Altwerger & Flores 1986).

The whole language premise behind not loading content study with activities is as follows: *children learn through use—they learn language by using language the way their culture uses it, and they learn science by doing science as scientists do.* Whole language teachers who understand this premise know that anthropologists do not do clever "follow-up activities" like conducting pretend interviews with a favorite informant when they wind up a study in New Guinea. They know that they themselves would not make dinosaur-shaped cookies in order to learn to multiply fractions, though they might use fractions to make size comparisons in order to understand dinosaurs better. They know that astronomers spend their working time investigating hypotheses about astronomical phenomena (or trying to get grants that would allow them to investigate these hypotheses). If they make models, they make them for purposes of investigation, not decoration. They do not spend their time writing stories about imaginary planets or making puppet shows on astronomy. And neither should children. No matter that such activities are fun. They are not honest science.

Thematic units are usually planned in advance by the teacher. Indeed some school districts distribute prepackaged units planned in advance by someone other than the teacher. Such preplanning means that the teacher (or the unit planner) has set the problems, identified the major ideas, organized the material, and found the resources. The teacher, that is, did most of the problem solving and therefore the learning. Theme cycles, on the other hand, give children the opportunity to do the kind of learning beginning teachers are always stunned by ("Now that I have to plan it and teach it, I've finally learned it!").

When children do science (natural, physical, or social), they pursue questions *they* are interested in; they set problems, find resources, and organize their own study. They enter conversations directly or indirectly (live or through books) with other scientists so they can learn how those other scientists answer other questions. They mess around with raw data, figuring out how to make sense of it, how to interpret it, and how to rule out competing interpretations. Teaching children who are doing science requires helping them generate new questions and new insights about questions *they* entertain, not entertaining them with a preplanned sequence of activities (Edelsky 1989a).

Topics for thematic units usually fit an adult view of what is appropriate for children. Either the topics themselves are innocent and appealing (e.g., bears, dinosaurs, pets) or they are "Disneyfied" and thus made innocent (e.g., treating Westward expansion as "Wagon Train" or studying other countries through the frame of quaint customs, sometimes, literally, to the tune of "It's a Small World After All"). Theme-cycle topics are sometimes the same as topics for thematic units (at certain ages, children are in fact interested in dinosaurs). But they are treated seriously (e.g., What arguments have people had about dinosaurs? Who won those arguments? How have those arguments been related to other arguments such as evolution versus creationism?). Sometimes, however, topics are the result of discovering what is *really* on children's minds (Harste 1989)—which can turn out to be, not dinosaurs, but nuclear war or parents being out of work or moral issues like what is fair (on the playground or in South Africa or El Salvador).

The whole language theoretical premise underlying which topics are pursued and how they are treated is *All knowledge is socially constructed.* Therefore all knowing is political. In an effort to promote critical literacy and thus to help children learn to read the world, not only the word (Shor & Freire 1987), teachers who work with theme cycles try—no matter whether the topic is overtly "political" or not—to show how the topic is related to other more general questions. They try to demystify social institutions by helping children investigate connections between surface facts and underlying social structures, between lived experience and structural features of class, gender, and race. They know that not making connections is as political as making connections.

When people distorted the open, organically integrated conception of open education so that it meant trivialized thematic units, they did so in a particular context. The late

1960s and 1970s were a time of both relative prosperity and of widespread social criticism. Values, traditions, politics—"the way it is"—were being questioned at every turn. Alternative institutions (communes, free stores, street theater) sprang up. In such a questioning context, perhaps the superficial approach to topics characteristic of thematic units did not matter so much. But times have changed. Whole language is gaining momentum when disparities between economic classes are widening, when the number of homeless people are increasing, when freedom to criticize is threatened by right-wing groups such as Accuracy in Media and Accuracy in Academia. Through the work of educational theorists like Apple (1982), Giroux (1983), and McLaren (1989), it has also become clearer that larger exploitative contexts have an impact on individual classrooms and relations within them, that increased democracy within classrooms must be accompanied by work on understanding and changing larger contexts. When whole language teachers miss the opportunity to study content seriously and critically today, when they substitute science activities for the doing of science, they are closing off one of the roads to a more democratic society. "We do not simply look for education that is gentler or kinder (or more fun or more interesting), but for education that fosters understanding, justice, and compassion, which emerge equally from the content and process of teaching and learning."[3]

The Current Scene

The picture of whole language has gained depth from looking at its historical background. One contemporary phenomenon in particular will add highlights. We are talking about the writing process. (We realize that the faddish term is process writing, but since its developers avoid that term, we will use

---

[3] We thank William Stokes, one of the thoughtful reviewers of an earlier version of this manuscript, for this felicitous phrasing.

the earlier term and the one they use—writing process.) In this section, we will show the compatibility of writing process and whole language. We will also discuss some subtle and intriguing ways in which they are different.

Writing process and whole language

In a sense, writing process and whole language are like regional dialects—they share major structural elements yet they have unique stories and idioms; they are mutually intelligible yet they reflect different birthplaces and identities.

Visitors to either writing process or whole language classrooms currently see the epitome of integrated (language) education. There is the same workshop atmosphere (Calkins 1986; Graves 1983). Children are engaged in work they own, they consult and offer an understanding ear to others engaged in similar work, and they take advantage of the rich store of literature available in the school and the community (Atwell 1987; Graves 1983; Hansen 1987). A major role for whole language and writing process teachers is responding to what the student is trying to do (Smith 1973; Graves 1983). To be sensitive to learners' intents, both whole language and writing process teachers "kidwatch" (Y. Goodman 1985). They also expand their own and learners' roles so that students become teachers of other students and of their teacher and teachers teach as well as learn about content (from students and other resources), about language and learning processes, and about their students' lives.

Occasionally, teachers in both kinds of classrooms directly teach content and skills—but not in the usual sense of "direct instruction." In these classrooms, teachers share tips on how to write and also information on whatever topic is at hand, all from a for-your-information stance ("From one writer to another, here's something I've learned that you might be interested in"). Such sharing happens in mini-lessons and individual and group conferences. Visitors to either of these classrooms see evidence in teachers' participation in literature studies and writing conferences that teachers are serious (but playful) readers and writers themselves.

Meaning (sometimes called content or information) has always been on center stage in both whole language and writing process orientations, but lately, content in the sense of social studies, science, and literature as content has moved closer to the spotlight. In either prototypical writing process or whole language classrooms, children work on projects where the goal is in-depth knowledge of a topic and where every possible language and nonlanguage resource is used to acquire that depth.

There is evidence in both sets of classrooms, as there is in published statements (Atwell 1987; Edelsky et al. 1983; Hansen 1987), that the teachers distinguish between genuine writing and writing exercises. In fact, one of the fundamental premises of both whole language and writing process is that children in school should be doing what real writers do—*writing*, not mock writing. Each supports the inseparability of form and function—the futility of teaching the meaning of a word when the word isn't being used in a genuine communication. Both honor children's "mistakes." Rather than seeing unconventional spellings, for instance, as bad habits that will impede further learning, whole language and writing process teachers know these are necessary to the learner and illuminating for the teacher.

Both understand the profoundly social nature of writing and learning to write. Either explicitly or implicitly, whole language and writing process beliefs include such Vygotskyan notions as:

1. All parties—teachers and students—influence what students can do in writing conferences and in turn are influenced by each other (i.e., there is a Zone of Proximal Development [Vygotsky 1978] in which people can be supported to do more collaboratively than they can individually—a circumstance that allows them, later on, to incorporate the collaborative effort into their own individual repertoires. One of the characteristics of the Zone of Proximal Development is that the "development" aided by the Zone goes in both directions [Engstrom 1986]).

2. Through learning which genres are favored for what purposes, who should write what, whose voice should be foregrounded, and other "lessons" made no less powerful

by being left unspoken, children appropriate important features of culture and can then use this learning to change culture (i.e., culture and history are transmitted in part through [written] language use and are transformed through language [Laboratory for Comparative Human Cognition editors 1988]).

3. People learn to write by attending to what they have to say in contexts where writing has particular meanings and where the writer has particular social relations with particular others. What is learned is thus a huge bundle—how to write plus what writing means plus what social relations accompany writing (i.e., writing is a cultural tool [a technology] that shapes and conveys thinking and that, with its historical and cultural particularities, constitutes a social practice [Vygotsky 1978; Street 1984]).

4. How teachers use written language *with* children affects what children learn about written language and how they should go about predicting, remembering, or interpreting to create texts (i.e., processes that eventually take place *intra*subjectively [within a person] first occur *inter*subjectively [between people] [Vygotsky 1978]).

To become either a whole language teacher or a writing process teacher, then, requires some major shifts away from prevailing beliefs. From believing learning is individual to knowing it is social. From believing written language is a system of parts with which people become skilled so they can use it later, to understanding that language is a major resource for making meaning, which people get better at using *as* they actually *use* it. From despising mistakes to respecting them. All this is no small matter. It constitutes a fundamental shift in one's total perspective, not just a change in "an 'activity' to 'do' with the class" (Hansen 1987, 193).

These are the major structural elements the two have in common. As with any "dialects," however, these two are also structurally different in at least one way. In their case, that difference concerns theory. Explicit theory in whole language is about the *nature* of language and language learning; explicit theory in writing process is about *requirements* for writing. Whole language is a framework that includes both an explicit theoretical base (about language and language acquisition) and pedagogical implications. It takes key characteristics of the way language is learned (e.g., that it's learned through real use with others, that hypothesis construction is a major part of the process, that meanings of social relations are acquired along with the language that accompanies those relations) as a "best model" for all learning in school, not just language learning. In other words, whole language is an umbrella—primarily an umbrella *theory-in-practice.*

Writing process is a framework that includes explicit attention to written language pedagogy and some generally *implicit* theory about the nature of writing. It takes key characteristics of the contexts writers rely on for their own growth (time [to write], ownership [of one's own writing], response [to one's own issues] [Atwell 1987, referring to Giaccobe]) and proposes "the workshop" (with time, ownership, and response) as a "best model" for all learning in school, not just the learning of writing. In other words, writing process is an umbrella—primarily an umbrella *pedagogy with implicit theory.* Whole language educators agree with that pedagogy though they begin with theory.

Writing process begins—but also ends—with "what real writers do." It doesn't explain children's meanings or actions in terms of the nature of written language or the theoretical relationship of writing, reading, and language, nor does it make a theoretical *analysis* of the role of language in learning or in life. The beliefs about language development we attributed earlier to both whole language and writing process can be found stated and explained explicitly in whole language tracts (see Edelsky 1989b; Edelsky & Draper 1989; Goodman & Goodman 1981; Harste et al. 1984). But theoretical statements must be *inferred* from writing process texts.

This somewhat subtle distinction between a theory in practice on the one hand and a pedagogy with implicit underlying theory on the other, is reflected in each group's selection of heroes. Which people outside of education are cited again and again in published statements and at presentations? Whole language authors usually choose linguists, semioticians, sociolinguists, anthropologists—that is, researchers and theoreticians who study language and child language. Writing process authors more often choose writers—that is, people who work at the craft itself.

If choice of outside heroes—a mark of identity—is related to theory, so is each "dialect's" evolutionary changes. Without an explicit theoretical tie between writing and reading, writing process either ignored reading at first or treated it as pedagogically separate from writing. (See Calkins 1983 for an example.) When writing process did begin to take account of reading as a process and to make connections between writing and reading, the reasons given were curricular, the reading process was presented as one of making meaning through separable strategies, and the instructional suggestions relied on sophisticated gimmicks like posing secret questions (Calkins 1986). In more recent statements, writing process educators have forsaken gimmicky external motivators and are now consistent with their new (and whole language's old) intent to capture what readers (not just writers) do when they read (not just write). (The New York City teachers working with Calkins and Harwayne, for instance, are themselves part of literature study groups, as are their students [Harwayne 1989]). Even so, current writing process reasons for rejecting basal readers are empirical (i.e., basals are not what readers *read* [Hansen 1987]); no theoretical explanation is provided for why readers fail to choose basals.

It is not the case, however, that if writing process was only about writing at the start, whole language was only about reading. From the beginning, whole language educators have looked at children's writing as well as their reading because whole language theory pointed to the similarities in reading and writing; that is, reading and writing were in the same theoretical category—language. Thus, young children's invented spellings (Read 1975) and their writing (Harste 1980) provided evidence for whole language beliefs about children's meanings and their language abilities. Therefore, whole language educators saw the value of writing process pedagogy from the start. Indeed they learned from writing process teachings a more profound pedagogical meaning for their own whole language theory of learning language through actual use, and they welcomed writing process as being whole language in spirit and adopted it as methodologically congruent with whole language theory.

Both whole language and writing process call for empowerment of teachers and students. Indeed, participating in either a whole language or a writing process classroom does have empowering consequences. After all, when teachers reject packaged, so-called instructional materials in favor of literature, real resource materials like thesauruses and almanacs and nonfiction texts (vs. textbooks), they take back control of at least some of their teaching. When students can shape their own topics and write and rewrite their own lives instead of marching through materials to the beat of scope and sequence charts, they gain a dignity that comes with being in control of their learning. Nevertheless, empowerment has had a somewhat different meaning for whole language and for writing process.

At the beginning, when whole language teachers took control of their teaching, they had to overthrow an established reading technology (basals, workbook commitments to publishers, packaged programs tied to tests with stakes attached, etc.). Before "literature based" was an acceptable or even widely known phrase, such an action had immediate political consequences (ask some of the teachers who were threatened with dismissal for insubordination if they didn't use the basal!). Those actions also had and still have the potential for demystifying the relation of big business and class ideology to curriculum and to teacher autonomy. Empowering actions stemming inherently from whole language theory, then and now, are politically threatening. And because they concern people as group members in work roles (the group called teachers), these actions give whole language–inspired empowerment a group meaning.

In the beginning, when writing process only meant writing, writing process teachers had comparatively little to overthrow. Writing process did not advocate doing away with spellers, language arts texts, and so on—though that was certainly an implication. At first, writing process was about "adding" a writers' workshop. While there were required language arts texts and spelling series, there were (and still are) no counterparts in writing that carry the same weight as that entrenched basal technology does in reading. Deciding to take control of one's teaching of writing, therefore, carried less political or economic threat within the big business of education. Empowering actions stemming from writing process in the early years when it was only about writing thus lacked the built-in potential for revealing teachers' roles in relation to the *structure* of the institution and the larger society. Writing process empowerment for teachers, then, is bound to have a more personal meaning than a teachers-as-a-group meaning.

As for students, however, writing process and whole language tend to aim for the same kind of empowerment. Most often, each envisions empowerment as individual rather than social (Luke 1989). Barriers to achieving individual potential are seen as close to home—individual inhibition, perhaps. Or maybe impoverished education. In any case, these barriers are thought to be removable by focusing on what is also close to home—the individual, the classroom. When empowerment is seen as social and emancipatory, however, barriers to achieving individual potential are understood as larger oppressive structures operating on life close to home. To remove such barriers requires curricular attention to those oppressive structures as well as to individuals and classrooms. The difference between aiming for individual empowerment by itself and aiming for individual empowerment through social emancipation is political. (We must say here that, like it or not, aware of it or not, as educators we are all involved in a political project. We are either perpetuating existing power arrangements, encouraging reform while maintaining the underlying structure, or promoting change in the underlying structure.) Now neither whole language nor writing process guarantees a particular political stance. But unlike currently prevailing pedagogies, each also has an inherent *potential*, at least, for being politically progressive. Each already subverts "the system" by doing away with supposed language skills–based curricula and reasserting teacher autonomy. Each *could* do more to rid education of language-based weapons used to oppress people (e.g., each *could* organize to eliminate high-stakes tests). Each already encourages the use of students' home language and discourse (while adding to it). Each *could* elicit literate activity that has real-world consequences. Each already views choice of content (writing topics, topics for subject matter study) as not confined to traditional disciplines. Each *could* permit the asking of out-of-bound questions with the potential to "shake things up." That is, each *could* make it its business to examine critically what is usually taken for granted against criteria favoring increased justice and democracy. Unfortunately, from our perspective, very few whole language or writing process educators deliberately use this potential. Not many ask students or themselves any questions that might prompt either an investigation of serious problems or a sustained critique of accepted practices. But a few do. (See Altwerger & Flores in press; Edelsky 1989b; Graves 1989 as examples.)

We have made much of these "dialect" differences because they are so intriguing, not because they prevent communication. Indeed, we would hope others too would see the differences as interesting enough to warrant talking about. Such a conversation could help us all increase our awareness of the issues and the possibilities.

What Whole Language Looks Like in the Classroom

■•

The picture of whole language we have been painting is well defined by now. We can add more color, however, with some scenes from actual whole language classrooms. We have made no deliberate attempt to represent a broad spectrum. No matter which whole language classrooms we would have chosen, such a spectrum would have appeared anyway. That is because no two whole language classrooms are alike. Each one differs considerably from all others in the way theory is realized in actual day-to-day practice. In part, this is due to whole language teachers' responsiveness to the overall social and cultural context of their teaching situations. The specific community which the school serves, the cultural, linguistic, ethnic, and class backgrounds of those particular students, and the nature of the local school system itself are all factors that whole language teachers consider in developing their programs. But the differences among whole language classrooms exist for an even more basic reason: *there simply is no uniform set of practices prescribed by whole language theory.* Teachers who know the theoretical bases for whole language agree on a particular instructional stance and a set of principles that guide their practice. But the way a teacher fills out this framework with particular materials, curricular plans, schedules, and classroom organizations will depend on the specific circumstances surrounding each classroom.

While whole language teachers are thus eclectic in their use of instructional strategies and resources, they are most

certainly not eclectic in their theoretical frameworks for instruction. They are not whole language in the morning and
skills based in the afternoon. They do not conduct literature
studies at ten o'clock and monitor workbook practice at
eleven. Though the practices seen in individual classrooms
vary, the underlying theoretical stance is unwaveringly
consistent.

Given the great variation among whole language classrooms, we will refrain from describing some nonexistent
"ideal." Instead, we will try to convey something of the range
of possibilities through describing some actual classroom
scenes.

Scene One

THS WEKS SPESHOLS proclaims the ad on the wall in the
small classroom that has been transformed into a supermarket. Next to that ad are others clipped from Albuquerque
newspapers. Labels mark the various departments (produce,
meat, dairy, post office). There are also labels identifying
what will be found on each shelf (cereal, cleaners, canned
goods, etc.). In the produce department, next to the scale are
student-made signs with pictures of apples, bananas, and
other fruits pasted on them and prices per pound written un-
derneath. Clearly, functional, meaningful, appropriate print is
everywhere.

It is immediately apparent that everything in the room is
child oriented—made by children, written by children, owned
by children, arranged by children. Items lining the shelves
and filling the display counters have either been brought
from home (empty cereal boxes, toothpaste boxes, plastic toy
vegetables and fruits) or made by students (meat made from
clay, painted the appropriate colors and wrapped with plastic). The toy cash register is filled with play money and child-
made money. Shopping carts have been made from chairs
with wire baskets attached, and are easily pushed around the
room.

The great attention to detail contributes to the realism of the supermarket. There is a counter near the cash register that holds coupons collected by the cashiers (these will be sorted later). In a corner of the room behind one of the counters is an office where the price list is kept, should labels or prices be missing from the items or shelves. As in many New Mexico stores, there is a small post office complete with flag, post office boxes, and a scale for weighing letters. The careful planning of the environment is reflected in a large poster entitled "Plans." On it are "get sack receipts," "make a scale for fruits and vegetables," "bring empty cartons," "make play money." There is also a picture book about the supermarket for use as a reference.

And everywhere there are children—busily reading labels, filling their carts with goods, counting out change at the register, checking prices in the office, weighing produce, reading ingredients to decide between cereals, sweeping up spills. The activity bears a remarkable resemblance to life in any real supermarket, and includes the reading, writing, computing, and talking that takes place there. Each child plays the role of someone who works or shops in supermarkets, and each emanates competence and confidence in fulfilling that role. There is a poster on one wall where children sign up for different roles each day, so that they experience the social structure from all perspectives.

If visitors look hard they can find the teacher. She is circulating around the room, asking the stocker for certain items, asking shoppers about their choices, and coaching the cashier with an impromptu mini-lesson on giving change from a dollar bill. At one point, she stops a shopper who is about to leave the store (car keys in hand, assisted by a packer to help her put the bags in the trunk). She whispers to the shopper that the meat the shopper bought smells spoiled and asks her what she thinks she ought to do about it. The shopper looks perplexed as she tries to think of a solution to her problem. Through some further questions about her rights as a consumer, the shopper herself decides to return the meat to the meat counter. When the butcher does not respond satisfactorily, the shopper complains to the manager, who courteously returns her money.

These students who read and write so competently and easily in this environment are not gifted first or second graders. This is a resource room and these are kindergartners and first graders who have been assessed as being "at risk" for learning to read and write because, presumably, they have language development difficulties or delays. In this classroom, however, their language development (both oral and written) exceeds everyone's expectations. Though none of these children would say that what they are doing in the supermarket is learning to read and write, that is, in fact, a strategically planned goal of the program. As in the real world outside school, all the reading and writing in this classroom are embedded within a social context and fulfill some important function. Literacy is not an end in itself but a means for accomplishing ends. Apprehension about learning to read, which partly derives from conscious attention to the learning process itself, is eliminated. Learning to read and write is both part of and by-product to learning and studying about the world.

This is a learner-focused classroom in the fullest sense. While the teacher's plans included some kind of study of the community, the students were the ones who chose the supermarket as the neighborhood establishment to study. They made repeated trips to the store with their class and their families. They formulated questions to ask, took notes, and later discussed every aspect of the supermarket "culture" as they constructed their environment. They became acutely aware of the necessity and functions of print both at the supermarket and as part of the planning and decision-making process in the classroom. Their ideas, concerns, and interests guided the project.

This classroom is not merely learner focused, however. It is also problem focused. While the children chose the supermarket topic, the teacher helped shape it. She instigated "trouble," telling the shopper about the rancid-smelling meat, or perhaps on another day making sure some shoppers had less money than others for buying the items they needed. The troubles were planted in order to study how such problems are solved in the local supermarket and to question both the problems themselves and the solutions in the light of rights, responsibilities, and fairness. Throughout, these "at-risk" children were remarkable in their ability to think analytically and critically about these issues.

The teacher in this program (Vicki Robinson, Eugene Field Elementary School, Albuquerque, New Mexico) has a solid understanding of language and language development. Her goal was to help her mostly low-income black and Hispanic minority language students learn and use language as a powerful tool for controlling their lives. The paradox is that although that goal required deliberate, diligent work from all concerned, it was achieved seemingly without effort.

Scene Two

The fifth-/sixth-grade classroom at Silvestre Herrera School in Phoenix, Arizona, is small and windowless. Except for a sink and a closet, the room has no architectural extras. It is loaded, however, with media—books, newspapers, magazines, tape recorders, and video equipment. Bookcases block off a corner for read-aloud sessions where everyone sits close together on the floor. But the variety of other activities that go on simultaneously occur "in public" with no physical barriers to screen out distractions. On this morning, some of the students are reading, some are working on stories or articles they'll be publishing, some are working on social studies or science projects they have initiated (like studying and making rockets, studying ancient Egypt, or investigating mystics). At a rectangular table near the middle of the room, one fifth grader and three sixth graders with their teacher, Karen Smith, are taking part in the opening session of a literature study on *The Endless Steppe*, by Esther Hautzig. This is a fictionalization of Hautzig's family's exile to Siberia during World War II. It follows young Esther in a forced labor environment as she and her family struggled to stay alive. With exquisitely poignant details, Hautzig tells a story of a grandmother who refused to give in to despair and of the strength of this family that sustained them all through their terrible ordeal.

This first session of the literature study group lasts for

nearly twenty-five minutes. It begins with the children talking about parts of the book they found noteworthy and the teacher taking notes on their comments. Later, the teacher will use the notes in formulating an assignment for the next session and in evaluating the children's participation in the literature study. For now, looking down as she takes notes allows her to avoid eye contact with the children so that they will talk to each other and not to her.

LISA: Where's that part? It's where she's in Siberia and she meets her friends. From the start I could see not only character change but story change. It was like, at the start, she was like a little girl. She knew she was rich but she wasn't that snobby. And at the end, she had to deal with a lot of things but she started noticing that they had other needs, not just material [needs]; they needed love to get through the war.

ROBERT: And when her father was called to the front line, she lost that—what was it, a thirty ruble note?

OTHERS: Uh huh.

ROBERT: And she started getting the coal and the wood for the fire and went to the market and sold the bread for twenty rubles and then she told her mother she wanted to make money so they could buy food. She wanted to get a job, but her mother didn't let her.

MARCELLA: But at the end she does. She started knitting and stuff.

ROBERT: She started with that old lady who couldn't knit on account of her hands.

MARCELLA: No, she started with the lady who had a daughter who was sick.

ROBERT: Oh, right.

MARCELLA: Yeah, and as part—to cheer her up, she asked Esther to knit a sweater.

TERE: In the book, I saw a big change of character 'cause in the beginning she was rich and then when they took her to Siberia she didn't like it there and—

ROBERT: She started adapting.

TERE: She got used to it and she *kind* of liked it because she had friends. It reminded me of *The Upstairs Room* 'cause she didn't have any friends at first.

(After about ten minutes, the teacher enters the conversation.)

LISA: I think the mother's manners toward him really made a big appearance [impression] or whatever on the daughter.

MS. SMITH: She dignified him. She treated him as a human being, regardless of what he had on, and he seemed to respond to that.

MARCELLA: She gave him confidence because, you know a person like that could be shy. I thought she gave him confidence that they wouldn't laugh at him.

MS. SMITH: It was interesting to me why they even put that character in there. I thought—well, maybe because it was really true—but I couldn't figure out why they put that character, the bum, in the story. I didn't see where it added to it or enhanced the story in any way other than maybe what you're saying here. Maybe that was the point. I hadn't really thought about it that way. Maybe it just shows one more time the mother maintaining her values from Poland even though she had been transposed to a different place and conditions were poor. Maybe that's it.

MARCELLA: *I* thought, like Lisa was saying, it was the value of love and everything. I thought *that* was the point she was making there [by putting in the character of the bum].

After another five minutes, Karen Smith opens the topic of what the assignment will be for the next session. Up until now, the book was read for pleasure and discussed without preordained parameters. From now on, parts of the book will be subjected to close rereadings; discussions in the three remaining sessions will focus on how the author crafted the text.

MS. SMITH: There are a lot of possibilities for this book. I don't know if we want to go back and look at the war, or if we want to look at some special events in detail and see how the author got them across. Do any scenes stand out in your mind? Like the cattle car stands out in my mind. I had real strong feelings in that one.

TERE: I like the end—the first sight of him when she was waving. It just got me. I almost started to cry. You think of all the things that she's been through. You put yourself in her position and what you'd be doing—

LISA: And like how old was she when they took him? Twelve?

MS. SMITH: It's got a lot of potential for drama, just because of how intense the feelings are. I don't know if we could sort out, you know, how we've done before—just make the diagram and find those critical elements and how she coped. We could look at the events to see what Esther's doing in each situation, to see how she's handling it. Because in the end she doesn't want to leave Siberia. And that just blows your mind. Why wouldn't she want to get out? But I think you've hit on it: it was the love, the human condition, the relationships.

In the end, the children choose to study the character of the grandmother. The teacher formulates the assignment: "How do we get to know her? How does Hautzig make her stand out?"

Like the kindergartners in the previous scene, these students too are not in a classroom for gifted children. On the contrary. Theirs is a classroom that could well have contributed to the killing statistics we all know. Below the poverty line, low-status ethnic group, home language (or own first language) other than English—these Hispanic fifth and sixth graders could be the ones who fail, the ones recommended for special education, the ones who eventually drop out. Instead, they are reading *The Endless Steppe* for study and each is concurrently reading at least two other pieces of literature for fun. They lead their own discussion at the beginning, couching some of their ideas in a discourse they have learned in past work with literature in this class ("I could see not only character change but story change"). They spontaneously tie one text to another ("it reminded me of *The Upstairs Room*") and think aloud with their teacher about the function a particular character serves in a story ("*I* thought, like Lisa was saying, it was the value of love and everything"). Sometimes, they work out an insight into a character, as Lisa did in describing what she called the grandmother's inward eye.

LISA: You have to have an inward eye. Like if you want to laugh you look back on something. That's an inward eye. Her grandmother did that with her granddaughter. She would say "Yeah, I remember your grandfather, the way he used to treat his flowers." And you *live* on that. She had an inward eye for the grandfather and she did sort of live on it. When she wanted to teach her granddaughter something she would have that inward eye for her grandfather. She would say "treat things with care" and then she'd go "remember how your grandfather did." Just remembering; that's the inward eye.

MS. SMITH: And she was really *living* on the memories. That's what kept her going.

LISA: That's what I was saying. "Living" is like laughing, crying—you're remembering when you do that.

In other sessions on other books, children in this class analyze devices the author used in crafting a piece of literature: "When I went back over the prologue, there's the wheel, right at the beginning," comments one child in a discussion of the theme of cycles in *Tuck Everlasting*.

What these children do not do, however, is answer questions to prove they can find details, take notes in literature logs to show they have complied with the assignment, or read aloud to prove they can read. Instead, in the act of working out their ideas together in these discussions, they reveal the results of their reading more clearly than they would by taking even the best test imaginable.

In the literature study discussions in this whole language classroom, the teacher does not ask questions to test comprehension. Instead, she assumes that each participant is a competent sense maker who brings a reasonable and defensible set of ideas to the group. Instead of evaluating the children's comments, she adds to them, encouraging a conversation rather than an asymmetrical pseudodiscussion in which the teacher appraises each student contribution. Karen Smith's contributions frequently "lift the level" of the discussion: in a session on *Prince Caspian*, for example, she comments, "So you're saying that voice is a symbol for [civil] rights." She often offers frames and ways of talking that children learn over time and that can help them move more deeply into story, craft, and the reasons for writing. In a subsequent discussion on *The Endless Steppe*, she tells the literature study group: "Instead of just saying 'grandmother really loved him,' we see grandmother pressing the dress with her hands in anticipation of seeing him; we see her blowing the dust off his hat. It's getting to the exact event with the specifics of the love." And later: "That's why people say writing is so important. It's not just to communicate feelings. Sometimes it helps you sort out your inward eye and make sense of life and feeling. So maybe by writing this down, every little event evoked a new feeling in Hautzig and kept it going. So writing may have served more than just a way to communicate to *us*."

For their part, the students feel responsible to come to the group prepared. It is likely that some have already wrestled with the legitimacy of their ideas and, in the wrestling between their own interpretation and anticipated reception, reached beyond their prior interpretive abilities. They do not, however, come to the group expecting the teacher to tell them whether they are right or wrong. They expect to participate in a genuine conversation about literature, in which the teacher can also say what she knows, argue a point, and wonder about something she didn't understand. In the various conversations—the silent internal ones with internalized others, the semiprivate ones between friends before and after the study sessions, and the "official" ones during study sessions— new voices, new viewpoints are added. The goal is to come to learn ever more interesting ways to understand how a piece of literature (and literature generally) is constructed—to understand *how* it means.

Such a goal is not achieved by treating literature as material to be exploited for the purpose of teaching reading (although real reading is indeed "taught" here). Nor is this literature study a mere supplement to some other reading program that *really* matters—for instance, a basal program. Literature study in this whole language classroom exists so people can immerse themselves in a piece of literature and then study it so that future immersions are even more meaningful.

The children are not grouped according to reading level. The day after a literature study is finished, the group disbands and, with other students, the former members pick new books and form new groups. The books are not assigned. The four who read *The Endless Steppe* chose to do so. They chose that book from a large library selected for quality and student appeal, not for readability. A variety of arrangements (buddy reading, assisted reading, reading aloud) are used to help some readers experience the literature. No one is told to put a book back because it is too difficult or the group is too advanced. This classroom is one big literacy club (Smith 1986), and everyone wants to—and does—join.

Scene Three

It is late October but the desert sun still turns modern school buildings into furnaces, so the blinds are drawn in Elena Castro's first-grade Spanish-English bilingual classroom at Dool Elementary School in Calexico, California. Despite the heat, the metaphorical classroom climate is comfortable and energizing. Children's work covers every inch of bulletin board space. The walls sport six-foot long strips of butcher paper containing statements about what the children already know, what they want to know, and what they're not sure of about spiders (the topic of the current content study). A few days from now, the lists will be updated. Now, they document "the collective knowledge" to date, as Ms. Castro calls it (Flores, Kaczmarek, Romero & Kirksey 1983). Some of this knowledge comes from what children knew from outside and what they reorganized through talking with classmates in school. Some of it is the result of reading (or having heard someone read aloud) and then discussing fiction and nonfiction about spiders. Much of it is what the children have figured out or still wonder about based on their observations of the collection of spiders in jars around the room.

This morning, we come in during journal time. A few children who have already finished writing and drawing today's entry have chosen a book to read from the class library. Making observations for another science project, recording critical reflections in literature logs, or working at cooperative learning tasks at the math workshop would have been other choices for early finishers. Most, however, are writing and drawing about self-chosen topics in whichever language they choose to write in. As they work, they talk to those around them. This talk is almost always an important adjunct to their writing—adding information, soliciting or giving help with conventions, gossiping about who is being drawn or written about. As they finish their entries, they turn their journals over, the signal that they are ready for the teacher to read and respond to their entry.

Nancy turns her journal over and soon Ms. Castro is crouching beside her desk. She pats Nancy's shoulder and says, "Bueno, mija. Léeme lo que has escrito" (Well, my little one. Read me what you've written.). From her entry (IOT-GUNMGAFVRTA), Nancy reads, "Yo tengo una amiga favorita" (I have a best friend). Elena Castro responds by writing on Nancy's journal, saying each word slowly as Nancy watches: "¿Quién es tu amiga favorita?" (Who is your best friend?) Nancy knows that if she can remember tomorrow what Ms. Castro just wrote, she can choose to make tomorrow's journal entry a response to this question. They talk for a minute about best friends and then Ms. Castro adds, "Acuérdate. Que vas a aprender a escribir y leer como un adulto mientras escribes como una niña y te fijas bien en cómo yo te contesto" (Remember. You are going to learn to read and write like adults do by first writing your way and by watching and figuring out how I respond to you.).

The teacher moves on to Daniel. He reads his entry to

her. Just as she is about to ask him to watch as she writes and reads aloud her response, he interrupts. "You don't have to read it to me. I can do it myself." He grins. So does his teacher. He reads her answer while she is hugging him, each soaking up the pleasure of the other.

Ms. Castro goes to Hector, who has been referred to Special Education. Hector has written AOIIAIOAIASA. Later, Elena Castro tells us that she had been worried about Hector; his seemingly random strings of letters had appeared particularly bizarre. Still, she begins the routine.

MS. CASTRO: OK, Hector, léelo. (OK, Hector, read it.)

HECTOR: La policía vino a mi casa (The police came to my house.)

Suddenly, she notices that perhaps the random letters are not so random. Except for the lone consonant at the end (as in *casa*), these are the vowels, in order, in Hector's statement. With mounting excitement about her hypothesis, she asks "¿Y qué más pasó" (And what else happened?) Hector answers: "Se llevaron a un ratero" (They took a robber away). She tells him to write it. He does: E EAOAUAEO.

Again, Elena Castro grins and hugs a student. But this time the student is not aware of the magnitude of what he has done. This time, the teacher's delight is also in what *she* has learned: Hector, the misdiagnosed "learning disabled" child is probably not disabled at all. He is indeed learning how written language works (he figures it is one letter per syllable), but he has begun with the vowels instead of the usual early choice of consonants. He has taken a major step in coming to know the alphabetic nature of Spanish and English (Ferreiro & Teberosky 1982).

Journal writing in this classroom serves several functions. It constitutes a social event in which children can interact using both oral and written language at once. Each mode of language augments the other so that the always social, always contextualized nature both of talking and writing supports the development of each (Dyson 1988). The teacher's decision to use journals interactively (Flores & Hernandez 1988; Staton et al. 1988) and respond to the children's entries rather than to use them as private diaries (another legitimate alternative with its own benefits) permits her to make personalized contact with each child every day. Moreover, because she responds to children's ideas rather than to their spelling, punctuation, spacing, or handwriting, journal writing time is safe. Children can take risks, can stake out the territory covered by a new hypothesis, can try out writing in a language they don't speak well, can deliberately and knowingly experiment.

When this teacher responds to the children's journals she reads out loud as she slowly writes her response. Such a practice offers the child countless simultaneous demonstrations (Smith 1981) about the ways speech and writing are and are not related. The demonstrations provide the "input" from which the child can then generate hypotheses about some subsystem of written language. In the course of responding (and offering demonstrations), this teacher also occasionally demystifies for children the instructional aspects of their joint interaction while matter-of-factly articulating her own faith in their learning. This is what was happening when, for example, she said that Nancy would "figure it out" by continuing to write herself and by watching adults write.

The daily journal-writing time in this classroom is also a stage on which each child acts out his or her conception, that day, about how written language works. Because Elena Castro knows the work of Ferreiro and Teberosky (1982) and others who study early literacy, she is a sensitive listener, one who can interpret the nuances of the performance against an informed theory (i.e., who can "kidwatch" [Y. Goodman 1985]). So when Hector displayed his hypothesis that written language is composed of syllables and each syllable should be represented by a vowel (an admittedly unusual but nevertheless still sensible hypothesis), Ms. Castro could appreciate it as an hypothesis, relate it to the research she knows on the nature of children's hypotheses in written-language acquisition, and begin acting as an advocate to change the label affixed to Hector.

Journal writing in upper-grade whole language classrooms affords similar opportunities. When older children write long journal entries to carry on a relationship in writing with their teacher, they too display hypotheses about everything from how to spell a word to how to gossip or complain in writing. Upper-grade teachers, too, write back by responding to children's meanings, often talking about themselves in return. In these relatively intimate written exchanges, upper-grade teachers also sometimes have a chance to see that children diagnosed as disabled on the basis of how they do exercises are not disabled in how they communicate in writing (i.e., in how they really *use* written language).

All of the children in Ms. Castro's first grade this year are Hispanic, but not all are Spanish dominant or even bilingual. Therefore, when literacy events permit children to interact extensively and informally with each other and to make their own groups (rather than *be* grouped, as in high-, medium-, and low-reading groups), there is opportunity for considerable cross-language interaction concerning written texts and the writing system itself. In this classroom, such interaction occurs frequently during journal time. In other bilingual whole language classrooms at other grade levels, it happens at other times. In some, it is during mixed-language literature study sessions: for example, English speakers and Spanish speakers in a study group might discuss the same book all have read in English, but they discuss it *with each other* in each one's dominant language; what allows the students to make sense of what each other has said are a common referent, heavy contextualization, profound intergroup goodwill, and a strong sense of belonging to the same learning community. Cross-language interaction might also happen during group project work where documents are investigated. Or during mixed-language, whole-class conferences on children's writing. Or it happens as it did in a different first-grade classroom where the teacher was conferring with a Spanish-dominant child about what she was going to write. The child said, "La niña está jugando en los columpios" (The little girl is playing on the swings). She hesitated a long time: how should she begin? Her "monolingual" English-speaking Anglo friend leaned over to help, pointed to the alphabet above the chalkboard, and said partly in Spanish "it's the *ele*, the *ele*" (Spanish for the letter *L*). In these classrooms, and in Elena Castro's classroom, biliteracy is an advantage, not a problem.

Scene Four

"Wanna read with me?" Her ponytail bounces in time with her steps as she takes her friend's hand and goes off with him to pick out a book. These first graders move between an open space pod and two portable trailers in rural-suburban Eldersberg Elementary School in Carroll County, Maryland. Their teachers are six members of "the first-grade team." Right now, we join the children in the areas supervised primarily by Mary Katsafanas and Barbara Cohen. Ms. Katsafanas and Ms. Cohen are off in different parts of "their" spaces, working with children. Other children are involved in different activities. Some are reading alone on the floor; some are at their desks hunched intently over a book. Others are reading in quiet corners, leaning against the wall. A trio is lying on the floor, turning the pages of a big book and reading it aloud together while one of them points to the print. A few pairs are scattered around, reading to one another or reading together. One child jumps up to read something to a friend; they giggle while pointing to the page. Some fifth graders are also in the room reading to some of the first graders, both older and younger ones seemingly enjoying the attention they are getting from each other. There are also one or two children whose books are open but who have stopped reading in order to record ideas and reactions in their reading journals. It is DEAR time (Drop Everything And Read time) and reading is certainly what is going on here.

Nobody asks the teacher, "What's this word?" Nor does anyone seem to be struggling. One little girl, however, leans over to ask the boy sitting nearby (who happens to be labeled "learning disabled") to help her figure out a word. Together they predict several possibilities until they settle on one that makes sense in that context and seems reasonable given the spelling. The little girl thanks him and they both go back to their own reading.

On the floor nearby, a newcomer (a boy who had experienced some difficulties learning to read in a different classroom where he was placed in the low basal group) is sitting with two little girls. One of them hands the boy a predictable book by Mercer Mayer, encouraging him with "Here, I bet you can read this book." With help from his new classmates, the boy begins to read the book. Occasionally, one of the girls (in a tone reminiscent of her teacher) encourages him to "say what would make sense there" or "just skip it." They laugh together at some of the pages; when they get to the end, the boy smiles with great satisfaction at what he just accomplished. The girls gleefully congratulate him. He asks if there are any other books like this in the classroom. One of the girls jumps up to find him several others by Mercer Mayer. The boy takes them eagerly.

Off to the side, one of the teachers and a child are discussing *Little House on the Prairie.* The child has brought this book to the conference to talk about her reaction to the part where the Ingalls family becomes severely ill. After listening intently to the child's lengthy comments, the teacher tells her about a time when she and other members of her family were sick, and how alarmed she had been when her own mother had not been well enough to take care of her. Together, teacher and child discuss how frightening it must have been for the pioneers who had no medicine, doctors, or hospitals available. The little girl says that she would like to live on a prairie like Laura and Mary, but she'd like to have a doctor nearby as well. After the conference, the teacher remains to write a few notes about the girl's reading progress.

Though DEAR time is only a small part of the overall day in this classroom, it serves some important purposes. Students develop their own interests and tastes in literature, learn to appreciate the range of literature available to them, and, most importantly, have a sustained amount of time every day simply to read. Children select from a wide range of genres and are free to read for a variety of purposes. Some read to research a topic of interest; others read plays that they will later perform; some explore a particular author by reading all of his or her works. Whatever their personal agendas for reading, the children are able to enact them and thus to maintain ownership over their reading.

DEAR time is not a silent time and this classroom is not a silent place. A low but productive buzz pervades. Children are expected to select their own books, read alone or with others (silently or aloud), and simply enjoy themselves with books. Despite the constant hum, children do seem engrossed in their reading; nobody needs to be reminded to read. Although some children may take a few minutes out to comment to someone else about their book (as adults often do with their spouses, roommates, and so on), everyone is acutely aware of respecting one another's time and space.

Reading in this room does not have to be a solitary act. The teachers know that students can transcend their own individual capabilities as readers when reading together with others. There is no ability grouping here either. Though students have a sense of the various reading strengths of their peers, they do not define themselves or others on the basis of reading level. Reading is simply not an arena for competition. Instead, children are anxious to share their favorite books with others; they readily give and accept help from their peers; and they include everyone, regardless of proficiency, in their spontaneous groupings. No one is considered a nonreader.

Like other whole language teachers, Mary Katsafanas, Barbara Cohen, and their four teammates (Lauren Hunter, Debbie Francis, Tammy Richards, and Jane Leonard) know what they know and what they don't know. At the time of our visit they were increasingly comfortable with how they were making their language arts curriculum compatible with a whole language perspective on language learning, but they were still struggling with how to approach content. And like other whole language teachers, they were actively trying to learn more—studying professional articles together and taking graduate coursework that would help them increase their understanding of theory and heighten the sensitivity and theoretical appropriateness of their practice. Equally important, they were using interactions with their students as data, analyzing them in the light of their changing conceptions of language and learning. On this morning, Mary Katsafanas confides that through her more informed participation in conferences with individual children, she is learning more than she ever knew about details and ranges of reading strategies and of children's reading tastes. She remarks, in fact, that though she has taught for eighteen years, she never really knew her students until she made the transition to whole language. She is particularly pleased with the quality of information that she can now relay to parents about their children. The teachers also speak of how they have learned to trust the children and to trust the learning process. In a sense they are right, but they downplay their own significant contribution (as the ones who plan for that process to operate unimpeded) when they maintain that the love of literature as well as the utility of written language are the *real* teachers in this classroom.

Scene Five

Except for not having any windows, this is a dream of a kindergarten classroom. It is huge, carpeted, and generously equipped (mostly by the teacher rather than by public funding) with the following: a sink; a microwave for baking; a black-and-white houndstooth-checked couch salvaged long ago from someone's garage and now bordering one edge of the space used for whole-class discussions; two tape recorders (one near a reading area so children can record stories and books they read aloud, and one that is usually playing some classical music at low volume near a big open workspace); huge wooden blocks for building secret hideaways, boats, and castles; a typewriter; a computer; "grown-up" maps, globes, microscopes, and other scientific tools; paint; clay; musical instruments; a library of children's books; dress-up clothes; a set of encyclopedias; and various live animals (fish, turtles, a snake, hamsters, newly hatched chicks). In one corner, an art gallery displays Jason's paintings and drawings in this week's one-person show. Poems children have brought in hang from the ceiling. Years ago, parents built a loft complete with suspended bridge, slide, and climbing pole. That loft has now served Chris Boyd's kindergarteners for fifteen years at two different schools. This year, in the kindergarten at Roadrunner Elementary School in Phoenix, Arizona, it stands off to the side of the room. Big as it is, it is nevertheless dwarfed by the bowling alley–sized space.

Though the room is entrancing and the loft is spectacular, for sheer impact-value, neither can compete with a "simple" request from six-year-old Nathan. Everyone is sitting close together on or near the couch. Chris Boyd has just finished reading one of James Marshall's stories about two hippopotamuses, George and Martha, who are friends. "Let's do an opera of it," Nathan suggests. An *opera?!* Our chins are on our chests! Surely the other kindergarteners won't know what he is talking about. Certainly the teacher won't be able to accommodate the request. But wait. What's that she is saying?

CHRIS BOYD: OK, who wants to be George?

SEVERAL: Me, me, me.

CHRIS BOYD: OK, Nathan. Now remember; as a hippopotamus, you're the first of your species to go up in a hot air balloon. How would you be feeling?

NATHAN: Um, happy. Oh yeah, he said pr...proud. Um, I'm, I'm, I'm proud.

CHRIS BOYD: OK. Sing it.

Fluently, Nathan's voice booms out, as though from his toes, in a made-up tune: "A-a-a-ah-h-h-e-e [I] am so proud." The teacher then asks who will play Martha. Several girls volunteer but cannot think of what to sing. Lisa can, though. With a tune sliding downward at first and then rising to a high pitch at "best" and "friend," Lisa as Martha sings a clear, thin "George, you are my best friend." Chris gets Mark, Terri, and Jo to play the part of the hot air balloon.

CHRIS BOYD: Now, remember, you've got a hippo sitting inside of you. How do you feel?

MARK: Flattened.

TERRI: You're too heavy.

OTHERS: Ugh.

CHRIS BOYD: OK. What will you sing?

MARK (*Singing in a deep monotone*): Get out of he-e-e-r-e.

TERRI, JO, AND MARK: Get out of he-e-e-r-e.

Chris turns to the remaining fifteen children. Some are to be flowers (the story takes place on a spring day). Some are to be

the wind. Some will be the grass. She gives the flowers a background trill; they will sing simultaneously with George,
Martha, and the hot air balloon. The wind-children decide to
sing "oo-oo-oo." The grass will sing a swishing tune after the
wind's "oo-oo-oo" blows through. Within a matter of five
minutes, the parts have been parceled out, the tunes somewhat invented, and the opera begins. In another minute, it is
over but then it is repeated with five other children taking on
the leading roles.

How do these kindergarteners know what an opera is?
Chris tells us that she played some tapes for a few weeks,
talked about the different kinds of art that go into operas,
and showed the chldren how to *sing* a story by making up
tunes and singing "The Three Little Bears" in all the voices
herself. Since then, the children occasionally suggest making
an opera of a read-aloud story or an anecdote a child tells.
Chris says the suggestion is almost always acted on in the
same spirit it was offered—that is, spur of the moment. No
preparations, no rehearsals, no costumes, no final performance for an audience.

Drama happens in the same way: in response to a child's
request, with immediately repeated "performances" so that
the roles can be rotated among all who want to try them on,
and with little fanfare. Of course, any teacher knows that
such spur-of-the-moment activity is hardly spur of the moment. That is, the ground has to be well prepared before such
shoots can "spontaneously" appear. The preparation in this
case comes from Chris Boyd's beliefs about language and
learning, which are reflected in all areas of the curriculum.

From the first day of school, these children from working-
class to middle-class homes are asked to do before they can:
that is, to write before they write legibly, to read before they
"decode," to use adult maps before they read maps, to take
observational notes on science experiments before they can
take notes, and so on. Their efforts are not just "cute"; they
are taken seriously because they serve purposes for the individual children or for the class as a whole. For example, if a
child wonders whether an absent child should be asked about
the whereabouts of a lost object, Chris will tell her to write it
down as a reminder. And when the absent child returns, the
written message is in fact consulted.

Every day, then, during writing time, story time, project time, and clean-up time, children are expected to *become* competent by being competent. Moreover, they are expected to be teachers of each other—to look to each other for suggestions on how to solve problems in writing, reading, webbing, note taking, cutting, measuring, and so on. Thus, even if some children remain less confident in their own abilities in other contexts, when they are all together in this class, a we-can-do-it ethos sweeps them all along; and having done it, they begin to learn how to do it. So when Nathan suggests doing an opera, no one says, "I can't."

If part of preparing the ground is to arrange things so the children can get used to feeling competent, another part is to make it commonplace for them to play with language. In this classroom, children play with language at scheduled times, at unscheduled times, as the focus for long blocks of time, and also as something snuck in for just a second when something else is the focus. They make up lyrics to familiar tunes, nonsense rhymes, chants, raps, riddles, jokes, and wisecracks, sometimes by following their teacher's lead and sometimes by initiating the inventions themselves. On this particular day during whole-class sharing time, two children tell jokes and riddles. On other days, in the middle of a writing or free-choice or math jobs time, Chris may get everyone's attention so a child can tell the entire class the good knock-knock joke he has just told her. In fact, for a while this year, knock-knock jokes were so popular that children were asked to choose knock-knock joke partners and write down each other's jokes.

The children are also used to transposing—taking a thematic refrain and fitting it into other contexts. For instance, children might focus on the sour-grapes stance in Aesop's *Fox and the Grapes*, find other stories in which characters don't get what they want, and have those characters mouth a sour-grapes bit of dialogue—when the bear in one version of "Gingerbread Boy" failed to catch the gingerbread boy, he might have said, "He'd have ruined my appetite for honey, anyway." None of this is planned to teach symbolic language or comprehension of the main idea or detection of homonyms. All of this language play occurs simply for the fun of it.

Because this teacher is tuned in to the aesthetic qualities

of language, she highlights the rhymes, alliterations, puns, and imagery that pop into or are inserted deliberately into her own talk. The children, then, come to learn that their classroom is a place where language play is welcome, where some of that play (e.g., their made-up songs) helps them bond as a community, and where the norms of that community include being a competent participant. In other words, every day in countless ways, the ground is prepared for a harvest of language play.

One such harvest occurred in a discussion that took place on another morning. A group that was supposed to have been making a map was having trouble working together. At the sharing time, the teacher asked the whole class to describe the problem as they saw it. After several contributions, Monty's metaphor, given credence by the teacher, sparked a new way to conceptualize and solve a group-process problem.

MONTY: It's like, it's just like they're all little pieces and they aren't coming together.

CHRIS BOYD: What do you mean by little pieces?

MONTY: You know. Like a puzzle. Like the pieces are spread out on the floor.

CHRIS BOYD: Like, what are the puzzle pieces that you're talking about?

MONTY: Our ideas, the ideas.

CHRIS BOYD: Well how do we get the pieces to come together?

DARREN: You have to talk.

CHRIS BOYD: You mean if Mike talks to Max will that make their pieces come together?

VALERIE: No, Max has to listen.

JESSICA: Yeah, if Mike talks and Max listens, it's like a magnet and it pulls their pieces together.

In this case, all that went into increasing children's ability to use the aesthetic qualities of language on the spur of the moment was harvested for an instrumental, instructional goal: problem solving. But there are even more frequent harvests in this classroom when the playfulness—the joys, the pleasures, and the fun everyone derives at the moment from playing with language—is an end in itself. When Natalie and Jessica listen to Grofe's *Grand Canyon Suite* and giggle that the section where the musical rain is just beginning reminds them of words like *click, drip*, and *splat*, when children make up raps and songs and sing them together for days on end, and when everyone agrees with Nathan that yes, let's do an opera—spur of the moment, absolutely *no* preparation—then we know there's been some remarkable preparation indeed.

Scene Six

"Hey, this came from a cup!" Scrunching in to get a better look, his second-grade classmate is dubious. "How do you know?" But the first boy has reasons. "See. The edge is rounded, nice and smooth." The dubious one isn't convinced. "So maybe it's a plate." But the first boy supplies the clincher. "Check it out, Dude. See. The design's only on the *outside*."

These two boys are at a Pottery Shard Center, searching through a box of shards to find just the right piece. Another boy at this center is looking through a book, trying to confirm his guess that black shards were used for cooking. They and nine other second graders in this Chapter One Resource Room found the shards on their school playground. When they first discovered them, they and their teachers decided to investigate where the bits of pottery came from and whether there had ever been Indians living there. The two-teacher team, Karen Dockstader-Anderson and Lori Steinberg, invited an archaeologist to come in as a consultant. Dr. Bronitsky accepted the invitation but agreed to talk only once and then only to fifteen of the forty-five grade one through five children who come to the Chapter One Resource Room at Alameda Elementary School in Albuquerque, New Mexico, each day. In that talk (audiotaped so the other thirty could also learn from it), he told them that the school was, in fact, built on an Anasazi Indian ruin and that archaeologists would approach other sites similar to this one as puzzles to be reconstructed, literally, bit by bit.

Today, two second-grade girls have gone to the "Bronitsky Says" center to listen to that tape. They have searched through their folders to find the questions they wanted their student representative to ask the archaeologist in person. Since all representatives did not have a chance to ask all the questions they had been entrusted with, the two girls still do not have satisfactory answers. Therefore, they are now listening to Bronitsky on tape, trying to see if some snippet of what he said applies to their questions. Each time they think they have found something, they press pause, transcribe or take notes, press rewind, and continue listening.

The other second graders have also taken out their archaeology folders and have moved off to various centers. Each folder contains the student's work and a check sheet with a list of centers. (Students do their own record keeping as to centers attended and work tried and accomplished there.)

Some of the other children are working at the Interactive Bulletin Board. Right now, this board sports a current map of the Albuquerque area and the invitation: "Bronitsky said there used to be fifteen pueblos in the Albuquerque area. There are only three left. Can you find them? What do you think happened to the other twelve pueblos?" One child writes on a post-it "THAY DID BECUS THAY GOT MESALS AND THAY GOT SIC AND DID." At the History Center, a boy is viewing a film strip and listening to a tape. Periodically, he stops the tape to write down a date and event on a note card. When he is finished, he will give it to the teacher to put on the timeline between 1400 and 1500. Two girls at the Native American Homes Center are looking at a Telex screen with a slide of a Pueblo woman at the door of an adobe dwelling. They can hardly believe the tape so they replay it. Yes, they heard correctly; though the Pueblo men built the homes, it was the *women* who owned them. Heads together, hunched over in delight, they note this tidbit in their archaeology journals. Two boys join them as the slide-tape show presents the information that some Indians today live in pick-up trucks instead of homes. Why? the children want to know. They offer several hypotheses to each other, then decide to ask the teacher if such a shift in housing can be a topic for whole-class discussion tomorrow. Other children have chosen other centers: the Poem Center, the Messages in Stone Center, and the Quiet Center.

This day occurs toward the middle of the theme cycle called "A Dig in Our Own Backyard." The study was prompted by the children's interest in the shards found on the playground. The overall question that started the study was: Was there an Indian Pueblo where Alameda School is now? Bronitsky's affirmative answer to that initial question could have ended the study. Instead, his visit provoked further study. Moreover, once the curriculum came to be strongly focused on what the children were recovering from the dirt, the playground finds became even more interesting. Prompted by the daily finds, the intellectual mine provided by the archaeologist, and the excitement of finding out that they were sitting on top of the remains of a past civilization, the children's questions multiplied.

Mostly, these questions concerned the people who had been there (Where did they come from? Where did they go? How did they live? Did they have gardens? Did they use bows and arrows? Did they dance? What language did they speak? Did they write to each other? Were they happy?) and the pottery they had made (How old is the pottery? What do the designs mean? Why is it on the playground? How was it made? Who made it? Can we make our own?).

The questions were "live ones" for the children; they were not simply the teachers' questions elicited from school-wise children. These child-owned questions provided structure and organization to the entire study. Unlike many centers planned to motivate children and to arouse interests, these centers were planned to *satisfy* interests. They took shape in order to help children answer their own questions once emerging questions became more clearly articulated.

As children's own purposes drove their study, so did they drive reading and writing within the study. This was due in large part to the many contexts within the theme cycle that provided real reasons (i.e., reasons other than "to comply with the teacher's asignment" or "to prove I can spell Anasazi") for reading and writing. For example, because Bronitsky had valuable information and children wanted that information to help them answer their own genuine questions, and because his information would only be accessible to a few for a short time, the children *had* to find ways to make the most of his limited consulting time. They needed to write and consolidate questions, to read and rehearse these so as not to waste time once he arrived. In other words, these were *real* notes, *real* reminders to representatives, real language in *use*.

In the course of the study, children made up their own chants based on the model of chants taped by Indians. They maintained a steady concern with an archaeological way of learning, asking frequently and explicitly, "If we were archaeologists, what would we do next?" They spent long periods of time and came back again and again to issues of the life of the Anasazi, the importance of writing as a means of preserving history, the aesthetic and functional differences between pictographic and alphabetic writing, and the contrasts between modern pueblo life and Anasazi life. This last included consideration of the sensibleness of modern Indian ways as well as such questions as why modern Indians live in government housing, trailers, and pick-ups, how Anglo culture was imposed on Indians, and how the social problems of modern Indians are related to the history of Indian-Anglo contact.

At one point early in the theme cycle, when Karen Dockstader-Anderson asked the children what they knew about Indians, they told her this astonishing "fact": all Indians are dead. They said they learned this from TV westerns. (Apparently, this kind of misconception is not so unusual. Young Navajo children sometimes wonder who those people called Indians are, not seeing themselves as part of that category, since they themselves are Navajo and the Indians on television are Plains Indians.) When the teacher explained that Indians are very much alive and that people of Mexican descent are often part Indian, the most provocative issue emerged—the children's own identity. Since most were Mexican-Americans, this new knowledge meant that by studying the Anasazi, they could well be studying a part of their own history.

It must be noted that the children who sustained their interest in these issues at such a pitch and at such length were those eligible for Chapter One; that is, those who were failing—low income, low scores. They came to the room in same-grade groups, ranging from first through fifth grade. Each class, whether first or fifth graders, participated in the theme cycle and used the resources to whatever degree they could. This theme engaged all of them not because it was "graded" or because the study used "reading-leveled" materials but because it grew out of the children's curiosity about something in their own environment. It was not a generic curricular topic; it was a *situated* topic. Themes or units developed by committees, unrelated to the specific questions of specific children in specific locations, and handed out for use in Elementary Everyclassroom, USA, cannot generate this kind of genuine investigation.

This was also a serious study of content, not an accumulation of unrelated trivia or even of discrete "facts." It was a case of children really trying to figure things out as archaeologists would. They were using math, science, art, reading, and so on to help them with their own questions; they were not using archaeology as an excuse for "contextualizing" the skills or for "integrating" the other subjects. The study could have focused narrowly on culture (that seemingly apolitical way to consider minority populations). But because of these teachers' own political understandings, it was broadened. The minority culture was not seen as "suspended in air" but as changing, the changes clearly affected by contact with the dominant majority culture and political system.

These six scenes from whole language classrooms represent very different ways in which teachers enact theory in practice. And, of course, none of them represent the entire program for that classroom. For example, the supermarket role playing occurred for only a certain number of weeks, just a few days a week. What all these classrooms have in common, however, is the whole-language, theoretical-instructional *framework* from which the curriculum emerges. Whole language is a generative frame that can support a great variety of curricular choices. And it is this generative quality that returns the power of teaching back to the teacher and the power of learning back to the students—but with a new perspective on what teaching and learning are all about.

Where Do We Go from Here?

■●■●■●■●■●■●●■

We wonder where you, our readers, are now—what you
thought when you started this book and what you are thinking now. In the course of writing it, we have changed some of
our own ideas, modifying them as we struggled to find words
to express what we had *thought* was clear but what, when we
had to write it down, turned out to be fuzzy around the
edges. We hope you have begun to do the same—to sharpen
the image and fill in the spaces. We want so much for us all
to be able to distinguish whole language from what it is often
confused with—a new style for an old way of "getting
words," a fancy label for the old idea of teaching skills in
context, just another method. We want us all to know how
historical contexts make innovations that look alike have different meanings and consequences. We want us all to see
both the variability in practice and the uniformity in princi-
ple that are whole language. It is all of that together—distinc-
tive meanings, particular historical context, variable practice,
specific stable principles—that makes whole language revolutionary. And, of course, all along we have been wanting you
to join us, to extend the revolution—in substance, that is;
there has been enough of just spreading the label. We know
the satisfaction and the power that come to students and
teachers who have begun to learn and teach in whole language communities. All students deserve such a chance; so do
teachers—so do *you*.

We also want to offset the "counterrevolution," that

backlash both of co-opting and defaming that we mentioned at the beginning. Some of those who stand to lose something (e.g., income from skills-based materials or consultancies, status and legitimacy as experts on skills-based instruction, materials, research, etc.) co-opt the term. For example, publishers and consultants who have little knowledge of or commitment to a whole language theoretical base use the label to sell everything from basals to packages of basalized literature to workshops to videotapes. Others, meantime, take the tack of discrediting all of the work going by the name of whole language (whether theoretically valid or not).

We are not saying that whole language should be exempt from questioning, analysis, and criticism. We too are critical of much that goes by the name of whole language. But there is criticism and there is criticism. One kind—the criticism meant to help—has to be offered delicately, particularly if the practitioners are new to whole language. They are just beginning to understand the theoretical bases of whole language and at the same time are experimenting with significant changes in their practice. Of course, these shaky new efforts should be questioned, but gently—by those making the efforts and by friendly critics. More than being critiqued, however, they should be applauded—for the gutsiness they require, for the originality they entail.

Not so for those behind the sham "whole language" activity that bears that name only because some people in high places want their school or district to seem up-to-date. These higher-ups designate all the teachers—willing or not, knowledgeable about whole language or not—as "whole language" ("I dub thee whole language!"). However, it is not the imposed-upon teachers who deserve the criticism here; it is the higher-ups who deprive teachers of their professional autonomy. These people either understand whole language so poorly that they think it is simply behavior and thus can be dictated from on high, or they know full well that it is a way of thinking but they go ahead and try to exercise thought control anyway. And certainly, there should be no applause for the efforts of businesses that want to exploit a "hot label" (changing only their packaging, not the theoretical basis or the contents of what's in the packages) in order to cash in (literally). That kind of "whole language" (which is really exploitation) deserves clear, loud criticism from all sides.

We also agree that whole language theory (not only classroom work) should continue to be subject to critical evaluation. All along, whole language has been an evolving framework. It continues to change as a result of just such critique and new learning by whole language educators. Theoretical criticism by opponents has also served to sharpen the understandings of whole language educators. In other words, we welcome hard-hitting theoretical dissent. But outright discrediting is another story. What we mean here is the discrediting of whole language that renders it invalid with the "always" arguments ("we've always done that") or that trivializes it with the "just another" arguments ("it's just another resurgence of [fill in the blank]").

The most frequent of the latter type of arguments is that whole language is "just another" generic name for Progressive Education. This discredits, not because there is no relation between the two or because an association with Progressive Education is something undesirable. It discredits because, in the first place, it doesn't take whole language seriously enough to learn its theoretical distinctiveness from other progressive movements in education. And, in the second place, it often presents Progressive Education in unappealing caricature—romantic, anti-intellectual, permissive, promoting unprocessed "feelings," distrustful of "the book," viewing learning as the natural unfolding of a Rousseauistic child-flower in a garden, viewing teaching as no more than garden maintenance. Whole language does indeed grow out of Progressive soil, but such a derisive portrait fits neither whole language nor all the major progressives, past or present. Refusing to carve people up into separate cognitive, emotional, and social parts is hardly romantic. Instead, it reflects the best insights of cognitive psychology (Bruner 1986). Though Dewey's Progressive Education may have shied away from "book learning" (in reaction to the nineteenth-century tendency to teach through rote memorization from texts), the classroom scenes described earlier show just the opposite. They reveal an intimacy with books (rather than a distrust of them) and a willingness to engage intensely with ideas, analysis, critique—hardly anti-intellectual. Aside from its historical context, what sets whole language apart from other progressives is its theoretical base in a transactional, sociolinguistic model of language use and a social interactionist view of language acquisition. That theoretical base does not assume a lone flower-child unfolding in a garden sanctum. It posits an active, social child born into a web of relationships and conversations that started before she was ever born and that are now changed forever by her part in them. Nothing in whole language theory (nor in Dewey's, we might add) suggests that children's learning just unfolds. Instead, whole language argues that "teachers" (parents, siblings, schoolteachers) are vital—not for giving out-of-context lessons in an effort to instruct directly what cannot be directly instructed in the first place, but for helping neophytes with what the neophytes are trying to do. Nor does whole language's insistence that texts have multiple meanings mean that "anything goes." A transaction between reader and print *includes the print*. That is, both "parties" contribute, which means that only meanings that can somehow be traced to the print's contribution are plausible meanings. When we hear detractors claiming that whole language is "just another" example of educational romanticism, anti-intellectualism, and the like, we wonder whether they have read any whole language theoretical statements or seen any classrooms where practice is congruent with those statements. We wonder how they justify the use of criteria that make a close study of literary texts and firsthand research in whole language classrooms seem "soft" while workbook-dominated, dumbed-down curricula appear rigorous.

Discrediting may have the most immediate and dramatic impact. However, in the long run, co-opting may be the most insidious threat. Claiming (by naming) to have done what it hasn't, the huge corporate-governmental-bureaucratic-educational system passes off skills-based materials as whole language, skills-based classroom practices as whole language, skills-based ideas as whole language. Why bother, then, to learn about whole language when, with just a few minor changes in outward appearances, everyone and everything already *is* whole language? This is all too familiar. We have seen the language experience approach mistakenly identified as flash cards on a shower ring, and open education bastardized to mean dittos at "centers" in an open pod. If the co-opters have their way, whole language could well become a kit of questions that accompany grade level–assigned literature. *It must not.*

It is critical to the future of education (no, we are not being melodramatic) that whole language not be distorted, that it grow as the revolution it truly is, with its potential fully used for contributing to increased justice and democracy in the world. The first step toward that end is for more people to clarify their understanding of the theoretical bases of whole language and the differences between whole language and other educational phenomena. That is what this book is about. It should help people become more knowledgeably whole language, which, in turn, should

1. Allow them to offer students the best possible education.
2. Allow them to enjoy for themselves the benefits of being consummate professionals.
3. Give them more protection against opponents' discreditings.
4. Make them less susceptible to hucksters selling "whole-language-basal-snake-oil."

A book can only go so far, however. It can offer a long, detailed discussion of whole language as a framework but it cannot do the work of making that framework come alive, day by day, in particular classrooms. Only teachers can do that. And only teachers who do that can teach us all what the possibilities are.

A paradox: education (and society) is in trouble now; at the same time it has a chance to be the best it has ever been. For some, this chance in education is already being realized. These people know that, for them, a small revolution has taken place. Others could take the same challenging, empowering road. All it takes is vision, understanding, knowledge, hard work, and commitment—qualities good teachers have always had. The destination this time, however, is not arrived at through just *any* vision, *any* knowledge, *any* commitment. Where we're going is toward a principled practice, continually examined against a whole language set of beliefs about language and language learning—all in the service of a literate, educated, just society. We hope you will join us in taking that road. It makes a difference.

Bibliography

•■•

Allen, R. V. 1964. The language experience approach. In *Teaching young children to read,* ed. W. G. Cutts. Washington, D.C.: U.S. Office of Education.

———. 1976. *Language experiences in communication.* Boston: Houghton Mifflin.

Altwerger, B., K. Diehl-Faxon, and K. Dockstader-Anderson. 1985. Read-aloud events as meaning construction. *Language Arts* 62: 476–84.

Altwerger, B., C. Edelsky, and B. Flores. 1987. Whole language: What's new? *Reading Teacher* 41:144–55.

Altwerger, B., and B. Flores. 1986. Theme cycles. Keynote address, TAWL Conference, Tucson, Arizona.

———. In press. The politics of Whole Language. In *The Whole Language Catalogue,* ed. K. Goodman, Y. Goodman, and L. B. Bird. New York: Macmillan-McGraw Hill.

Altwerger, B., and V. Resta. 1986. Comparing standardized test scores and miscues. Paper presented at annual convention of International Reading Association, Philadelphia, Penn.

Altwerger, B., V. Resta, and G. Kilarr. In press. *The theme cycle: Creating contexts for Whole Language strategies.* New York: R. C. Owen.

Altwerger, B., and E. Saavedra. 1989. Thematic Units vs. Theme cycles. Workshop presented at CEL Conference, Winnipeg.

Antler, J. 1987. *Lucy Sprague Mitchell: The making of a modern woman.* New Haven, Conn.: Yale University Press.

Apple, M. 1982. *Education and power.* Boston: Routledge and Kegan Paul.

———. 1983. Work, gender, and teaching. *Teachers College Record* 84: 611–28.

Aronowitz, S., and H. Giroux. 1985. *Education under siege: The conservative, liberal, and radical debate over schooling*. South Hadley, Mass.: Bergin & Garvey.

Atwell, N. 1987. *In the middle*. Portsmouth, N.H.: Boynton/Cook.

Bakhtin, M. 1986. *'Speech genres' and other late essays*. Austin, Tex.: University of Texas Press.

Bloomfield, L., and C. Barnhart. 1961. *Let's read: A linguistic approach*. Detroit: Wayne State University Press.

Brearley, M. 1972. The practical implications for the teacher. In *Open education*, ed. E. Nyquist and G. Hawes, 336–52. New York: Bantam.

Bruner, J. 1983. *Child's talk: Learning to use language*. New York: Norton.

———. 1986. *Actual minds, possible worlds*. Cambridge, Mass.: Harvard University Press.

Bussis, A., and E. Chittendon. 1972. Toward clarifying the teacher's role. In *Open education*, ed. E. Nyquist and Hawes, 117–36. New York: Bantam.

Calkins, L. 1983. *Lessons from a child*. Portsmouth, N.H.: Heinemann.

———. 1986. *The art of teaching writing*. Portsmouth, N.H.: Heinemann.

Chall, J. 1967. *Learning to read: The great debate*. New York: McGraw-Hill.

Clay, M. 1975. *What did I write?* Auckland, New Zealand: Heinemann.

Cochran-Smith, M., E. Garfield, and R. Greenberger. 1989. Student teachers and their teacher: Talking our way into new understandings. Paper presented at Spring Conference, National Council of Teachers of English, Charleston, S.C.

Counts, G. 1932. *Dare the school build a new social order?* New York: John Day Company.

DeFord, D. 1985. Validating the construct of theoretical orientation in reading instruction. *Reading Research Quarterly* 20:351–67.

Dewey, J. 1900. *The school and society*. Chicago: University of Chicago Press.

———. 1916. *Democracy and education*. New York: Macmillan.

———. 1963. *Experience and education*. New York: Macmillan.

Dyson, A. H. 1988. Drawing, talking and writing: Rethinking writing development. Occasional Paper No. 3. University of California at Berkeley: Center for the Study of Writing.

Edelsky, C. 1986. *Writing in a bilingual program: Había una vez*. Norwood, N.J.: Ablex.

————. 1988. Living in the author's world; analyzing the author's craft. *California Reader* 21:14–17.

————. 1989a. Critique of content study. Paper presented at annual convention of National Conference of Teachers of English, Baltimore.

————. 1989b. Literacy education: Reading the word and the world. *English in Australia* 89:61–71.

Edelsky, C., and K. Draper. 1989. Reading/"reading"; writing/"writing"; text/"text". *Reading-Canada-Lecture* 7:201–16

Edelsky, C., K. Draper, and K. Smith. 1983. Hookin' 'em in at the start of school in a "whole language" classroom. *Anthropology and Education Quarterly* 14:257–81.

Edelsky, C., and K. Smith. 1984. Is that writing—or are those marks just a figment of your curriculum? *Language Arts* 61:24–32.

Eeds, M., and D. Wells. 1989. Grand conversations: An exploration of meaning construction in literature study groups. *Research in the Teaching of English* 23:4–29.

Engstrom, Y. 1986. The zone of proximal development as the basic category of educational psychology. *LCHC Quarterly* 8:23–42.

Ferreiro, E., and A. Teberosky. 1982. *Literacy before schooling.* Portsmouth, N.H.: Heinemann.

Fleck, L. 1979. *The genesis and development of a scientific fact.* Chicago: University of Chicago Press.

Flores, B., Amabisca, E., and E. Castro. In press. Sociopsychogenesis of children's literacy and biliteracy. In *The Mexican American child*, ed. A. Barona, L. Moll, and E. Garciá, vol. 2. Tempe, Ariz.: Bilingual Press.

Flores, B., and E. Hernández. 1988. A bilingual kindergartener's sociopsychogenesis of literacy and biliteracy. *Dialogue* 5:2–3.

Flores, B., K. Kaczmarek, T. Romero, and D. Kirksey. 1983. *Instructional strategies for language arts and reading.* Glendale, Ariz.: Glendale Elementary School District.

Fodor, J., T. Bever, and M. Garrett. 1974. *The psychology of language.* New York: McGraw-Hill.

Freire, P. 1970. *Pedagogy of the oppressed.* New York: Seabury Press.

Giroux, H. 1983. *Theory and resistance in education: A pedagogy for the opposition.* South Hadley, Mass.: Bergin and Garvey.

Gollasch, F., ed. 1982. *The selected writings of Kenneth S. Goodman.* Vol. 1 and 2. London: Routledge and Kegan Paul.

Goodman, K. 1968. The psycholinguistic nature of the reading process. In *The psycholinguistic nature of the reading process*, ed. K. Goodman, 13–26. Detroit: Wayne State University Press.

———. 1969. Analysis of oral reading miscues: Applied psycholinguistics. *Reading Research Quarterly* 5:9–30.

———. 1984. Unity in reading. In *Becoming readers in a complex society*. 83rd Yearbook of the National Society for the Study of Education, ed. A. Purves and O. Niles, 79–114. Chicago: National Society for the Study of Education.

———. 1986. *What's whole in whole language?* Portsmouth, N.H.: Heinemann.

Goodman, K., and Y. Goodman. 1981. A whole-language comprehension-centered view of reading development. Occasional Paper No. 1. University of Arizona: Program in Language and Literacy.

Goodman, Y. 1980. The roots of literacy. In *The Claremont Reading Conference*. 44th Yearbook, ed. M. T. Douglass, 1–32. Claremont, Calif.: Claremont Reading Conference, Center for Developmental Studies.

———. 1985. Kidwatching: Observing children in the classroom. In *Observing the language learner*. ed. A. Jaggar and M. Smith-Burke, 9–19. Newark, Del.: International Reading Association.

Goodman, Y., and B. Altwerger. 1981. Reading: How does it begin? In *Discovering Language with Children*, ed. G. S. Pinnell, 81–85. Urbana, Ill.: NCTE.

Graves, D. 1983. *Writing: Teachers and children at work*. Portsmouth, N.H.: Heinemann.

———. 1989. Keynote address at Elementary Section General Session, Spring Conference, National Council of Teachers of English, Charleston, S.C.

Gross, R., and B. Gross. 1969. *Radical school reform*. New York: Simon and Schuster.

Hall, M. A. 1976. *Teaching reading as a language experience*. Columbus, Oh.: Merrill.

Halliday, M. A. K. 1977. *Learning how to mean*. New York: Elsevier North-Holland.

———. 1978. *Language as a social semiotic: The social interpretation of language and meaning*. Baltimore, Md.: University Park Press.

Hansen, J. 1987. *When writers read*. Portsmouth, N.H.: Heinemann.

Harste, J. 1980. Examining instructional assumptions: The child as informant. *Theory into Practice* 19:170–78.

———. 1989. Paper presented at annual conference of National Council of Teachers of English, Baltimore.

Harste, J., and C. Burke. 1977. A new hypothesis for reading teacher research: Both teaching and learning of reading are theoretically based. In *Reading: Theory, research, and practice*. 26th Yearbook of the National Reading Conference, ed. P. D. Pearson, 32–40. St. Paul, Minn.: Mason.

Harste, J., V. Woodward, and C. Burke. 1984. *Language stories and literacy lessons.* Portsmouth, N.H.: Heinemann.

Harwayne, S. 1989. Informal presentation to administrators. Glendale Public Schools, Isaac Imes Elementary School, March 28.

Heath, S. B. 1983. *Ways with words: Language, life, and work in communities and classrooms.* Cambridge, England: Cambridge University Press.

Hines, V. 1972. Progressivism in practice. In *A new look at progressive education,* ed. J. Squire, 118–65. Washington, D.C.: ASCD.

Holdaway, D. 1979. *Foundations of literacy.* Portsmouth, N.H.: Heinemann.

Hudelson, S. 1984. Kan yu ret an rayt en ingles: Children become literate in English as a second language. *TESOL Quarterly* 18: 221–38.

Hunt, R. 1989. A boy named Shawn, a horse named Hans: Responding to writing by the Herr von Osten method. In *Writing and response: Theory, practice and research,* ed. C. Anson, 80–100. Urbana, Ill.: National Council of Teachers of English.

Isaacs, S. 1971. *The children we teach.* 1932. Reprint. New York: Schocken.

Laboratory for Comparative Human Cognition Quarterly Editors. 1988. Introduction: Comparing Piaget and Vygotsky. *LCHC Quarterly* 10:98–99.

Lamoreaux, L., and D. Lee. 1943. *Learning to read through experience.* New York: Appleton Century Crofts.

Lindfors, J. 1987. *Children's language and learning.* 2d ed. Englewood Cliffs, N.J.: Prentice Hall.

Loughlin, C., and J. Suina. 1982. *The learning environment.* New York: Teachers College Press.

Lucas, C. 1976. Humanism and the schools: The open education movement. In *Challenge and choice in contemporary education,* ed. C. Lucas, 169–91. New York: Macmillan.

Luke, A. 1989. Curriculum theorizing and research as "reading practice": An Australian perspective. Paper presented at annual meeting of the American Educational Research Association, San Francisco.

McLaren, P. 1989. *Life in schools: An introduction to critical pedagogy in the foundations of education.* New York: Longman.

Miller, G. 1973. Some preliminaries to psycholinguistics. In *Psycholinguistics and reading*, ed. F. Smith. New York: Holt, Rinehart & Winston.

Monaghan, E. J., and E. W. Saul. 1987. The reader, the scribe, the thinker: A critical look at the history of American reading and writing instruction. In *The formation of school subjects*, ed. T. Popkewitz, 85–122. London: Falmer Press.

Nyquist, E., and G. Hawes. 1972. *Open education: A sourcebook for parents and teachers*. New York: Bantam.

Ochs, E. 1982. Talking to children in Western Samoa. *Language in Society* 11:77–104.

———. 1984. Clarification and culture. In *Meaning, form, and use in context: Linguistic applications*, Georgetown University Roundtable on Languages and Linguistics, ed. D. Schiffrin, 325–41. Washington, D.C.: Georgetown University Press.

Peterson, R. 1981. Language experience: A methodic approach to teaching literacy. *Georgia Journal of Reading* 7 (Fall): 15–23.

Peterson, R., and M. Eeds. 1990. *Grand conversations: Literature groups in action*. Richmond Hill, Ontario: Scholastic-Tab, Ltd.

Piaget, J. 1967. *Six psychological studies*. New York: Random House.

Popkewitz, T. 1987. The formation of school subjects and the political context of schooling. In *The formation of school subjects*, ed. T. Popkewitz, 1–24. London: Falmer Press.

Postman, N. 1985. *Amusing ourselves to death*. New York: Penguin.

Read, C. 1975. *Children's categorization of speech sounds*. Urbana, Ill.: NCTE.

Rosenblatt, L. 1978. *The reader, the text, the poem*. Carbondale, Ill.: Southern Illinois University Press.

———. 1985. Viewpoints: Transaction versus interaction—a terminological rescue operation. *Research in the Teaching of English* 19:96–107.

Sacks, H. 1973. On some puns with some intimations. In *Sociolinguistics: Current trends and prospects*, Georgetown University Roundtable on Language and Linguistics, ed. R. Shuy, 135–44. Washington, D.C.: Georgetown University Press.

Shannon, P. 1989. *Broken promises: Reading instruction in twentieth-century America*. Granaby, Mass.: Bergin and Garvey.

Shor, I., and P. Freire. 1987. *A pedagagy for liberation*. South Hadley, Mass.: Bergin and Garvey.

Silberman, C. 1970. *Crisis in the classroom: The remaking of American education.* New York: Vintage Books.

Smith, F. 1971. *Understanding reading.* New York: Holt, Rinehart and Winston.

———. 1973. Twelve easy ways to make learning to read difficult. In *Psycholinguistics and reading,* ed. F. Smith. New York: Holt, Rinehart and Winston.

———. 1981. Demonstrations, engagement, and sensitivity: A revised approach to language learning. *Language Arts* 58:103–12.

———. 1982. *Writing and the writer.* New York: Holt, Rinehart and Winston.

———. 1986. *Insult to intelligence: The bureaucratic invasion of our classrooms.* New York: Arbor House.

Staton, J., R. Shuy, J. Payton, and L. Reed. 1988. *Dialogue journal communication: Classroom, linguistic, social and cognitive views.* Norwood, N.J.: Ablex.

Stauffer, R. 1975. *Directing the reading-thinking process.* New York: Harper and Row.

Street, B. 1984. *Literacy in theory and practice.* Cambridge, England: Cambridge University Press.

Taylor, D. 1983. *Family literacy.* Portsmouth, N.H.: Heinemann.

Teale, W., and E. Sulzby. 1986. *Emergent literacy.* Norwood, N.J.: Ablex.

Trabasso, M. 1981. On the making of inferences during reading and their assessment. In *Comprehension and teaching,* ed. J. Guthrie, 56–76. Newark, Del.: International Reading Association.

Veatch, J. 1968. *How to teach reading with children's books.* New York: Citation Press.

———. 1978. *Reading in the elementary school.* 2d ed. New York: Wiley.

Veatch, J., F. Sawicki, G. Elliott, E. Barnette, and J. Blakey. 1973. *Key words to reading: The language experience approach begins.* Columbus, Oh.: Merrill.

Vygotsky, L. 1978. *Mind in society.* Ed. M. Cole, V. John-Steiner, S. Scribner, and E. Souberman. Cambridge, Mass.: Harvard University Press.

Weir, R. 1962. *Language in the crib.* The Hague: Mouton.

Wigginton, E. 1979. *Foxfire 5.* Garden City, N.Y.: Anchor Books.